Beauty and Chaos:
Slices and Morsels of Tokyo Life

By Michael Pronko
Raked Gravel Press 2014

Beauty and Chaos: Slices and Morsels of Tokyo Life
By Michael Pronko

First paperback edition, 2014
Copyright © 2014 Michael Pronko
First English Edition, Raked Gravel Press

First Japanese Edition, Media Factory publishers, 2006

All rights reserved worldwide. This book may not be reproduced in any form, in whole or in part, without written permission from the author.

Typesetting by FormattingExperts.com
Cover Design © 2014 Marco Mancini, www.magnetjazz.net

ISBN 978-1-942410-00-3

Table of Contents

Part One: Fastidious Refinement, A Meticulous Love of Life

No Space Left Unmapped 3

Automatic Tea Ceremony 9

Floods of Advertising—On Sale Now! 15

What's Your Bag? 19

Life Delivered to the Door 23

Half Empty or Half Full? Walls of Bottles 27

Waiting to Blossom—Cherry Tree Maps 31

How I Ended Up Here 35

Part Two: A Beautiful Confusion

Frames of Emptiness 43

Clothing That Shouts—T-shirt Words 49

Standing Libraries 55

Reading the Signs 61

The Point of Point Cards 67

The Noisiest Time of Year 71

Ordered Around—Public Rules 75

The Delicate Ritual of Small Change 79

A Big Bowl of Japan 83

Part Three: Scenes from the Train

The Paperback-Cellphone hypothesis 91

The Pumpkin Train—Late Night Commuting 97

Hanging On the Meaning 103

The Ebb and Flow of Human Motion 109

All the World's a Stage-Train Platforms 115

Slideshow Lives, Glimpses Inside 121

Both Directions at Once, Change in the City 127

Tokyo's Million Marathons 131

No Time to Spare—Schedules 137

Part Four: Beauty and Chaos, Slices and Morsels of Tokyo Life

Souvenirs from the Land of Impulse—Don Quixote . 143

Elegant Eating—the Art of Chopsticks 149

What Goes Around Comes Around—Pachinko . . . 153

The Tradition of Banners 159

The Summer Whispers and Calls 165

Bathing in *Kanji*—Hanging Menus 169

Pink Power 175

Floating in a Sea of Words 179

Singing in the Rainy Season 183

Part Five: A Maze of the Mind

Up and Down and Down and Up—City of Stairs . . 189

A-maze-ing Tokyo 195

The Shiny and the Rough 201

Escalators to Heaven 205

The Love of Small Places 209

Around and Around—Going in Circles 213

Bonsai Buildings 217

Part Six: After Words

Seeing the City, Reading the City 225

The City Provokes Me—Why I Write These 231

Japan and Me 237

After Words and Thanks 243

Glossary 251

Dedication 259

Also by Michael Pronko 259

About the author 261

It was like a metaphor.
  Cees Nooteboom

You must stay drunk on writing so reality cannot destroy you.
  Ray Bradbury

Tokyo is an empire of signs.
  Roland Barthes

Tokyo is an empire of relations.
  Saiichi Maruyama

Confusion is a virtue.
  Chinese saying

Part One
Fastidious Refinement, A Meticulous Love of Life

No Space Left Unmapped

Maps are an essential part of life in Tokyo. Every bookstore carries a wide selection of city maps, tourist maps, graphic atlases for driving, walking, or train-ing, and map-laden guidebooks for everything from historical walks to shopping streets to bar hopping. Department stores post floor-by-floor layouts, restaurants hand out enticingly mapped flyers, and office building lobbies post diagrams as often as office numbers. Cell phones access on-screen maps, websites magnify and customize maps, while computerized navigation maps in cars and taxis even talk!

Then there are the train maps—of all the different lines, of the station interiors, of the station exits, of the train car doors most convenient to transfer at different stations down the line, and of the areas surrounding the exits. Racks offer glossy paper maps of the nearest *chome*. Then, once outside the station, there are those quaint, half-rusty metal maps clamped onto fences that show every small slice of nearby territory in hand-painted detail.

What kind of a city would spawn so many maps? I am not sure which amazes me more—the level of detail or their omnipresence. This peculiarly Tokyoite obsession is more than just practicality, I think. Of course, even the most experienced commuter or hardened shopper needs a map from time to time, but something more is at work with all these maps.

I notice this affection/obsession most often at the wide banks of ticket machines at stations. Plastered above the machines are huge megalopolis-wide train maps. The colors, ovals, balloons, varying marks, differing versions, brief annotations, and highly simplified lines all struggle to clarify the complexities of the train systems. These are not easy to use, of course, but people stand and stare longer than they really need to verify their direction. They seem to take pleasure in just following the flow of lines, considering alternative routes, mulling over the journey, and pondering how the immense sprawl of the city can be condensed into three white panels.

On the train, I always stand where I can see the diagram of train lines stretched over the door. They hang there not just for ease, but majestically, like a cryptic Buddhist saying over a wooden temple door. I notice other commuters also staring at these maps or gazing at the single-line list-map of station names. Rather than just whiling away a boring commute, they seem to be enjoying the accumulating passage of each station as they ride along. The map at times seems better than the city itself passing outside, or at least more comprehensible.

No Space Left Unmapped

On Tokyo's streets, I often see perplexed people searching for places. They surreptitiously check the map in hand against the concrete confusion of actual cityscape. Even normally reserved Tokyoites chuckle when at last they find the right place, sometimes even pointing with glee at the actual place that has appeared, finally, almost magically, right in front of them. When that happens, the map has worked its navigational trick, so that one feels like a world-class adventurer. Though Tokyo's territory is perhaps the most thoroughly gone over cartographically of any in the world, from an individual standpoint, it very often feels unexplored.

Part of that constant newness of Tokyo comes from its visual plane of surfaces, outsides, windows, side streets and odd cut-ups of space that make it hard to process. To get anywhere, the mind has to exclude the unnecessary and focus on the relevant. Maps reflect this mental process perfectly. They offer a kind of self-locating comfort—a reassurance through artistic simplification. The *Yamanote* line, which in fact coils around awkwardly like a dead snake, becomes a prim, perfect oval with colored lines spinning out in all directions like sunrays. The style is smoothed and rounded, almost cute. Some harried days, without that near-comic compactness, the city would just be too overwhelming.

After all, Tokyo is NOT a comforting city of straight,

easy-to-follow lines. Its logic, if there is one, is hidden deep. Yet, on maps, the city seems to make perfect sense. The jangled, frazzling chaos of the city appears neat and ordered. All is connected; all is positioned. The gargantuan proportions of the city can be taken in at a glance. Maps allow us to step back from time to time with a welcome two-dimensional abstraction.

Maps then are something like X-rays. They strip down the city to its essence and reveal its inner structure. They remove the bewildering surface distractions of Tokyo and let us see the city very differently. Maps trim away the extras to reveal the inner connections, and, more importantly, its intangible beauty. Maps offer an aesthetic sense of permanence amid the constant, at times aggravating, flow of trains, people, bikes, cars and construction. Maps remind us that the city, despite its ongoing self-renewal, has continuance, like a plant that grows back in the same way, no matter how often you cut it.

But perhaps the most intriguing part of Tokyo's maps is the smallest—the little red marker that says, "You are here." That point helps locate oneself in the middle of the hustle-bustle of the city with startling reality. No one ever really sees the city as a map does; even the tallest skyscraper offers only half-angled views and the street allows only baffling, too-human-sized perspectives. So whenever I look at a map of Tokyo, (and fortunately, I get to look rather often), I relish first the grand, impossible, top-down perspective, and then I search for that little red marker, that lets me think to myself, yes, I really am here.

Automatic Tea Ceremony

Whenever you need a drink in Tokyo, you need not walk far. Vending machines sprout up like metal mushrooms in every once-empty stretch of urban space. A lone vending machine poking up in the middle of a park, breaking up a block-long temporary construction wall, or set into the fence of a soon-to-be-developed plot of land would surprise no Tokyoite. The surprise is when you can't find one.

My first reaction to all these machines was how many, how ugly and how tacky-cheap they were. Cigarettes, condoms, alcohol, flowers, tickets and even rice can all be had at the drop of a coin and the poke of a button. Buying any of these from a machine seemed to be a symbol of the cold, distancing forces of technology and so-called convenience. These white boxes of wasted energy stood as a testament to the dehumanizing forced-feeding style of Japanese consumerism, just another way to con another 100 yen from my pocket and avoid wages for employees.

Gradually, though, I realized the genius of these brief, little pleasure centers. To stop and have a cold something at any of the white behemoths bolted into concrete corners and onto underused walls is anything but alienating.

Rather, in the midst of the mad flow of Tokyo, a slim syringe of cold tea is highly restorative. Stopping to suckle a canful of fluid helps to insert into the jabbering, adult conversation of commuting a pause, a breath, the open silence of a Japanese sentence that speaks volumes. In Tokyo, slowing the flow by stopping to take a moment for re-hydration or sugar loading is very needed at times.

What you really get for 100 yen, or 110 or 120 yen, is a cold, wet shiver of stationary comfort, or a warm-up in the cold when the machines switch to hot drinks, and a moment of quietude before charging back into the fray. If you were to completely stop in a café, say, it would be harder to re-start the engines and get going again. Drink vending machines are like the little cups of water handed to marathon runners as they pass by. They are comfort stations in the *ekiden* rush of Tokyo life. Grab one and run on.

Of course, you could do that at any of the *kissaten* coffee shops or small shops everywhere and anywhere in Tokyo, but that's different. Entering into the interior of another space, public as it is, means entering into a whole realm of conventions and obligations. The mere task of ordering an ice coffee sometimes just seems too much. Vending machines remain entirely outside of all social engagement. They are neater, quicker, smoother, and less trouble. Simple and satisfying, they sanction anonymity. They require no polite language exchanges.

That doesn't mean cold, distant and inhuman, however. The very simplicity is transformative; the clinking drop of the coin becomes a gurgling drop of liquid, the primal human intake, individual desire, pure self-centeredness. It is very human indeed, like a fantasy where one can stand and drink and relish the illusion of the importance of one's own personal inner narrative of need.

After all, the machine is only the outward symbolic front of human input. An entire network of social, psychological, economic, and technological complexity is contained behind the cheerful, bulbous front of drink machines. One night, I saw six men hefting a pristine new machine up a flight of stairs in a station. It took them about five minutes per stair, even with the special stair-climbing handcart they used. The vending machine was like a miniature pre-fab building, only more complex.

Caretakers of the machines come around during off hours, wheeling heavy stacks of boxed cans. It is also always a little shocking to see them open the machine for re-stocking or repair. Seeing the revealed innards, the sharply poised sprockets, the punched steel dividers and wild springy wires is almost obscene. We relish the normal covering up, the unexposed magic of the machine, the colorful membrane of functionality. Once the cover's shut, the machines have a cuteness and compactness that appeals to the heart of most Tokyoites.

Yet, the vending machine purchase is not really a loss of traditional, social interaction. It might seem the crude negation of the elaborate rituals of shared eating and drinking ceremonies or the chatty stopover along the ancient *Tokaido* highway, but the root is the same. What seems a little tacky, cold and impulsive is also very practical, comforting and spiritual. The blend of human and mechanical, ritual and relaxed, aesthetic and practical are as different as watching a historical drama on TV is from going to see kabuki at a theater. But at heart, vending machines are a kind of rough, commonplace reincarnation of the refined delicacy of that most Japanese of cultural expressions—the tea ceremony.

To me, this feels curiously spiritual, offering a hint of animism and the resignation of re-established ritual. Out of respect, and a kind of awe, for this mysterious production of pleasure, drinkers, coin droppers, lots and lots of them all over Tokyo, bow deferentially to the modern shrine to technology. To pick up the can from the black receptacle at the bottom of the machine, a respectful bow of the entire body is unavoidable. With the slim metal slot substituting for the wooden collection box of a temple, and the button and buzz substituting for a rope and bell, the machine seems to waken the hiding gods to hear our petty little silent prayers, as shrine goers do all over the country, and come down and out to enjoy with us a moment of fleeting delight.

Floods of Advertising–On Sale Now!

Every so often in Tokyo, I step completely into an advertisement. At least it feels that way when an entire train is engulfed in an all-over promotional campaign. When every single spot inside a train features one new product's image over and over, I know that once again, I have been swallowed up by the Japanese concept of *shinhatsubai*.

Shinhatsubai is a potent concept. A kind of advertising madness that springs from the world of commercial consumerism, *shinhatsubai* campaigns blanket the visual space of Tokyo with a peculiar kind of energy. In Tokyo's high-energy market, *shinhatsubai* stands as one of the most characteristic expressions of Tokyo's consumer mindset. In Europe and America, too, newness appeals, and sells, but in Tokyo, newness seems an obsession.

What amazes me most is how any new item of any sort can be put on sale? Where would it fit? Every shelf in every store in Tokyo is so jammed to rush-hour-like capacity with products and more products. There isn't even any room for more shelves, nor more stores either. So when I see the *shinhatsubai*, I wonder where anything could possibly fit.

Beauty and Chaos

Of course, old products have to be taken away. Retired or out-of-date products disappear quietly into obscurity, while advertising directs everyone's attention to newness. An entire product cycle of birth and death recurs over and over again, with each *shinhatsubai* advertising sounding like the over-enthusiastic pride of a new baby announcement.

Many products appear regularly or seasonally. A new style of beer is concocted at least every season, like some quarterly report on beer factories, despite beer being perhaps the oldest product in the history of civilization. Gum, lipstick, and video games, all constantly have the necessity of *shinhatsubai*. Every week or so bright new flavors, splashy new colors, and clever new ways to video-kill new characters appear in these ads.

Something about *shinhatsubai*, though, seems very different from stereotypical Japanese character. Normal people would never jump out and thrust their *meishi* name cards at you or shout wildly at you on first meeting. Just the opposite, Japanese are usually calm, quiet and reserved—exactly opposite to how *shinhatsubai* slaps you in the face with attention grabbing techniques.

The techniques of *shinhatsubai* advertising, too, seem unlike Japanese aesthetics. The lettering feels loose, wild and extravagant. The *kanji* seem to burst from the page, shooting up to the right or across the top with breathless

Floods of Advertising—On Sale Now!

excitement. For me, that electric kind of lettering feels so different from the graceful curves and elegant *kanji* usually respected in Japanese culture.

The smiles on the faces and the pose of the bodies, too, feel fake and contrived. Like with beer, there is simply nothing new in human bodies, but the nubile young women posed with enticing voluptuousness try hard to create the illusion of newness. The body language of *shinhatsubai* models conveys over-enthusiastic messages that lack the appeal of natural looks.

Then, there are the little give-aways. Key rings, folders, jackets, small boxes, and plastic containers, all sent for "free." Those little brand products further the advertising into other areas where the average advertisement could never reach—into homes, out on picnics, into cars, and deep in purses. The feeling of "*shin*" must disappear in all those places pretty quickly.

There is a backlash in Japan, though, too. Non-advertised goods have their own appeal and sense of elegance. Whether these goods are high-class or fureeta fashion, they refuse advertising to gain a kind of non-advertised notice. Their appeal lies outside of or beyond the predictable confines of shinhatsubai presentation. "I don't know that" becomes the alternative to shinhatsubai, and can be just as appealing.

All this newness seems the harmless diversion of

Beauty and Chaos

a commercial fantasy. The impression one gets from all the *shinhatsubai* campaigns is that products are constantly being created with tremendous novelty, yet, in reality, most products have only the slightest of developments. They just loudly label themselves "new." The emphasis of *shinhatsubai* is really not on the first *kanji*, *shin*, for "new" but on the last, *bai* for "sale." It just takes a lot of advertising energy to pretend otherwise.

What's Your Bag?

In Tokyo, most people carry more than one bag, often more than two. All over the city, well-designed store bags dangle from people's hands in what amounts to a huge, mobile, display of bag craft. Tokyoites always have a standard purse, work or school bag, but most days they also carry an extra bag from a store. The practicality of these bags is the least of it; the meanings, uses and quality are appraised and understood. You can see people's pride in strutting along the street with a good store bag—or two—or three—in hand. Bags are an essential part of Tokyo life.

In Tokyo, part of the pleasure of purchasing anything is the bag. Quality matters and quality is a carefully studied business. When purchasing anything at a store, Japanese wait apprehensively for their first look at the bag. Does it have a good handle? Is it laminated? How strong is it? Will the bottom folds become pushed out and bloated? Where and when can the bag be re-used? The quality, both of material and design, varies with the price of the store. Some stores overshoot their level by offering exceptional bags, but typically it's a perfect fit. People know they will be proudly using those bags many times for many purposes.

Every Japanese home has an area reserved for carefully saving these bags to be re-used. My home has four bag storage sections: one for cheap bags that could be used for trash; one for bags that are nice enough for close friends or self-use; a premium bag area for high-quality, well-designed bags to enhance small gifts; and lastly, a super-secret space for really superior bags to be used only for extremely special occasions, or perhaps never even used at all. I have an entire shelf in my office for received bags that can be re-used when lending students or colleagues a book, CD or other little item. Once a year or so, I sort through them and throw out the worst, re-folding the good ones and putting them neatly in order.

Some of these bags will be saved for years—waiting for just the right moment, the right gift and the right person to be given their bag "life" back again. Picking the right bag and returning it to the citywide bag circulation that runs through Japan like an alternate economic system is always a special pleasure. It can take considerable time before leaving the house to find just the right bag. Taking something "naked" would be embarrassing. Giving away a longtime favorite bag can be distressing, but receiving an unexpected great one is a pleasure.

Bags are practical and functional of course; saving and re-using them is part of the *mottainai* attitude of never being wasteful, one of Japan's most obdurate values. Choosing just the right one to re-use, though, is an important and tricky ritual. The crinkly sound of some bags makes them too noisy; others are too slippery or too thick. Some have a strange feel or do not fit what you are carrying or giving. The lettering, colors, tape over the top, handle, and "foldability" all interact for a complex set of considerations that match the perfect bag to the situation.

Tokyoites are careful about their appearance, so bags often match their outfits, in color, style or texture. In western countries, the thing inside is most important; any old outer bag will do. For Japanese, an extra store bag works like a small accent to what they wear, an important accessory, a statement. The coy passion for wrapping in public, knowing there is something inside, also creates an alluring intrigue. I always wonder what exactly is in all those bags. Bags make a statement with simple flair and a whiff of mystery.

Most of all, bags reveal how much Japan is at heart still very much a gift-giving society. The bags form an essential part of the gift-giving ritual. The levels and types of bags are as complex as the grammar of Japanese verbs for giving and receiving. Most beginning Japanese language texts for foreigners would do better to leave out the confusing lessons on verbs for giving and receiving, *ageru*, *morau* and *sashiageru*, which takes years to master in any event, and instead just put in drawings of appropriate bags for different social situations. Having the right polite language is always good, but giving a gift in the wrong bag is a major social gaffe. To avoid such embarrassment, people save bags for whatever contingency might arise in the complex system of gift-giving manners.

These bags are the modern version of the traditional multi-purpose cloth *furoshiki*: they wrap, enhance, carry, contain, hide, and show off. Bags replicate traditional aspects of Japanese psychology and culture with modern convenience. Compared to the purses, briefcases, and uniform schoolbags, which are obligatory *giri* bags that hold necessities, job stuff and serious things, these re-used shop bags are dedicated more to fun. They could be called *ninjo* (the opposite of obligation—human feeling) bags, filled with desired purchases, an extra possession, a small gift, or a borrowed item to be returned—in short, they are filled with humanity and feeling. Perhaps Tokyoites need to always keep those two realms separate and distinct.

I am sure, too, that if a huge earthquake ever hits Tokyo, as it is predicted to do, that all these bags will save lives. They would store things cleanly, distribute rice, protect feet, or carry water. In a post-earthquake world, with so many things sure to be lost, these millions of bags will still be performing their many practical and social functions for a long time to come.

Life Delivered to the Door

When I first moved to Japan, a friend gave me a huge microwave oven and the two of us carried it up the station stairs and crammed on to a rush hour train. The three of us—two foreigners and a huge box—took up a lot of room, so people really scowled as they stumbled around us.

During that first year, I hauled everything from large suitcases from Narita to overstuffed chairs from Shibuya to a heavy, old-style computer from Akihabara—all on the trains. I felt everyone staring at me with pity and contempt for using up more than my share of the public train, but I didn't quite know what to do about it. As an American, I was used to carrying everything in my own car.

Finally, I discovered the brilliance of *takuhaibin* delivery services and my problems were solved. It's a system I've come to rely on and marvel at. *Takuhaibin* trucks are everywhere. Every neighborhood street, mansion entrance and office building driveway has trucks stopping by off and on all day delivering packages.

Traditionally, of course, delivery has always been part of Japan's urban culture. In the *Heian*-era Kyoto of *Genji Monogatari*, love poems were sent all over the city from lover to lover. Now, though, in this age of materialism, everyone sends things instead.

What really amazes me is how the packages actually get to where they are going. In Tokyo, streets are like mazes and addresses like math puzzles. *Takuhaibin* delivery people, like modern-day samurai, act directly without hesitation—actually running, usually, right to the door. How millions of packages a day can move from one point to another without being lost is a kind of miracle. Packages are flowing constantly from place to place all over Tokyo, like blood cells, barely seen under the urban skin but essential to the life of the city.

The other day, I stepped down to the street to take a peek inside the truck. Though I embarrassed the driver, what I saw was an unbelievable level of organization. The various-sized packages were laid out in the back of the truck just like the various-sized houses and apartments along the route. I realized the entire city, the entire country, is completely mapped out, with every address entered in the master navigation system and the high-tech handheld computer module the drivers carry, just ready and waiting to be delivered to.

But if it was just practicality, the appeal would be limited. *Takuhaibin* also saves embarrassment. Carrying things on the train, as I used to, lets thousands of passing people see what you bought and where. While some

Life Delivered to the Door

consumers like parading a name-brand bag on their arm, most Japanese like their purchases to remain discreet. The bland safety of the *takuhaibin*'s dull brown paper allows anything to be privately sent and received.

Also important is that people can easily send a present to a friend, relative or colleague without the social complexities of actually visiting in person. Tokyoites may have moved away from traditional visiting rituals of the past, but they still like to send gifts. *Takuhaibin* keeps alive the customs of New Year's and mid-summer gifts, of sending thank-you and other purposeful gifts. Without *takuhaibin*, social relations would become even more distant.

Every day I see the delivery trucks going down my street, stopping at nearly every door. The driver must feel like Santa Claus, bringing some gift to everyone along the way. And inside all those houses, I imagine everyone, in a childlike state of expectation, unwrapping the packages and taking a look at what's inside.

But, for every action, of course, there's an equal and opposite reaction. *Takuhaibin* has its equally complex counterpart—an "undelivering" system. Every morning, Tokyoites re-wrap the remains of their things, not in brown paper boxes, but in trash bags, and set them by the curb. Then, the *gomi*, trash service—an "anti-delivery" system—carries off the used-up shells of all the goods back along the same routes and roads they were delivered.

Half Empty or Half Full? Walls of Bottles

Bars and restaurants in Tokyo resolve the problem of space in intriguing ways, but none more so than with bottles. Operating in a limited space, food, glasses, oil, silverware and bottles—in short, all supplies—are openly and directly displayed, rather than kept hidden back out of sight, as is more often the case in western countries. The most pleasing displays of all are the bottles.

I say that not because I love drinking (I do), but because of the size and effect. Bottles of liquor line the entryways, shelves, counters, and racks and even serve as dividing walls. These rows of bottles form an essential architectural feature. They define space, instill order and create atmosphere. Of course, there's often no other place to put things in Tokyo interiors, but the care, order and patterning creates a comforting illusion of openness that not only dispels claustrophobia but forms an essential part of the eating and drinking experience in Tokyo. They make a virtue of necessity in a visually rich, and very Tokyo, way. The aesthetic of the bottle is basic to Tokyo.

Beauty and Chaos

The long rows, labels pointed outward, give a strong sense of order and neatness. The bottle arrangements offer a pleasingly rounded transformation of square, angular space. Their patterns provide texture, variation, and visual distraction. A room filled with bottles arrayed on shelves is one in which a smooth, repeated pattern is presented and a harsh symmetricality denied. The line of well-wiped bottles calls and beckons with flowing lines, shaded depth, and repetitions of form that mesh into a pleasingly intricate illusion.

In some sake places, the bottles are kept in the fridge, but always with the labels front and center, tidy and waiting patiently to be ordered. Many places line the outdoor windows with bottles, beckoning to passersby. Places with a bottle keep system, which might be better called a "bottle take" system, array the bottles openly and obviously, the individual names written by hand on the bottles. These names disrupt the repetitive line of bottles with quirky writing that humanizes with individuality and warmth.

The display of bottles also extends beyond the purely textural and shows off a feeling of plenitude and wealth. The sheer number conveys power, potential and supply. "This place can satisfy any demand" is the message. The display of bottles conveys not only quantity but quality. They express the sophistication that comes from know-

Half Empty or Half Full? Walls of Bottles

ing culture—foreign or Japanese. Having a collection of foreign wine bottles is to have knowledge of those wines. Having a display of different whiskies implies a mastery of information and cultural detail. The bottles give the impression of never-ending supply—of drinks and of knowledge.

Traditionally in Japan, the store housing of barrels of sake has always been a sign of prosperity and social connections. Not only do shrines amass donated *sake* barrels, especially at the most important time of the year—New Year's—but also in homes a rare bottle from this or that brewery makes a treasured gift for display. Sending of liquor is one of the essential practices of the New Year's and summer gift giving season. Now, even if just beer tickets are sent, images of cans or bottles are lined up on the printed background of these tickets, as they are inside the gift boxes themselves.

Liquor bottles mean social connections, knowledge of different customs, cosmopolitan sophistication, and the ability to instantly relax. These social values re-assert themselves in the line of bottles in a restaurant with special force. The bottles become controlling and empowering containers of images of pleasure that hover over the inside like animated sentinels. Though the phallic nature of a wall full of bottles is obvious, the bottles are totems that are believed in, played with, handed back and forth, and integrated fully into the ritual of an evening. Everyone holds the bottle and pours for someone else. The group is symbolically framed by the bottles on the wall and symbolically reconfirmed by the bottle in hand.

The repeated patterns of lined bottles are an essential aspect of all commerce in Tokyo. All Tokyo stores—from the largest electric store in Akihabara to the smallest mom-and-pop vegetable stand—have racks of repeated shapes. The bottles are a special example, though. They dominate the space and give depth and meaning to the activities of eating, drinking and talking that take place beneath their overview.

Whether wine, *sake*, *shochu*, whiskey or beer, the lines of bottles communicate a comforting illusion, of the surety of repetition and the potential for free choice. From the long line of bottles, one has been chosen for one's own table. To have a bottle is to take part of the common storehouse of supplies, in short, to be part of a group. This appeals to the snobbery of being selective and the comfort of being participative. The repeated patterns of the bottles form an abstract visual pattern, but are part of the concrete world of experience, too.

Even the morning after, when the empties fill the plastic recycling crates outside the restaurants and *izayakas* waiting to be picked up, they fall into patterns more orderly than anyone might notice passing by them in the hurry of the morning.

Waiting to Blossom–Cherry Tree Maps

Looking for an obscure address in an unknown part of town, I found on my map in a Tokyo atlas a series of pink squiggly circles along a canal. I stared at these markers on the map as I walked from the station towards my destination. Only when I got close enough to the place could I see what the little pink circles were meant to represent: cherry trees, of course.

Maps of Tokyo are obsessively detailed and exceptionally clear. Computer-made maps chart the city with detailed accuracy at many levels of resolution. Tokyo maps display tangled chippings of land, complex numbered quadrants and the fascinating angled disorder of Tokyo's layout. Then, alongside the expected gray rectangles representing buildings, crossing signals, convenience stores, banks and McDonald's are page after page of these lively pink symbols of cherry trees all over the city.

What other country's maps would include cherry trees on maps that typically only delivery people, salespeople, walking addicts and the directionally challenged use?

Beauty and Chaos

Cherry trees, along with Mount Fuji, are one of the central icons of Japanese culture, so why would it be surprising to see cherry trees marked on maps of Tokyo? It shouldn't be, but it is somehow.

Most of the year, cherry trees are nice crinkled, snoozy grandparents of trees. Pink, a color that is excessively cute most of the year, becomes, as if in a fairy tale, a venerable, virile hue, with impressive gradations of serious red and dazzling white. It's not the kind of thing that maps in the west would ever convey—the seasonal color of trees. Yet, along streets, canals, streams and in parks are the maps indicating the probably rather exact position of cherry trees.

It seems strange too that they are put in pink, since the annual limited engagement of overwhelming spring color is so short. Yet, the maps have colored in those trees, right there in the middle of all the other unchanging spatial locators. It's as if cherry trees are equal in importance, direction and meaning to these other facets of Tokyo's appearance, as if nature deserves equal position with all the man-made markers.

Which, of course, they do.

Then, I thought, well, why not have cherry trees on maps? What other country in the world has flower reports nestled in after the news, sports and weather? What other country prints, on the front page of the newspapers, the expected dates of blooming south to north along

Waiting to Blossom—Cherry Tree Maps

the archipelago? All those TV news reports have maps of Japan dotted with cherry tree blossoms. I like the way a western scientific import, meteorology, is subverted by age-old eastern aesthetics.

Cherry blossoms seem to oppose maps in their fundamental intent. After all, cherry blossoms don't DO anything exactly. They aren't medicinal plants; they hardly produce many cherries even, inside Tokyo anyway. Though ancient maps were often works of art, maps in this day feel ugly and functional. Maps are always a means to some other end, shopping, sales, delivery, or finding a place. Cherry trees, in contrast, are ends in themselves; they are beautiful, pure and simple.

Maps, too, rely on spatial longevity, even though in Tokyo, stores succeed stores, banks change their names, and corners turn into pachinko parlors. The numbering, the streets, and the shape remain the same. Cherry blossoms, though, bring the timeframe of their several-week blossoming into this serious, reality-ordering plan. Those little pink dots infuse the map with a different sense of values altogether—beauty, renewal and brevity.

Looking at my atlas, I like to picture Tokyoites fleeing the delimiting gray boxes to just wander from pink circle to pink circle. Though I thought those pink circles were some cartographer's joke at first, I realized that they were serious. The map recognizes the importance of cherry trees. In many places, surely, the cherry trees have remained longer than anything else. I like a map that includes the wonderful unpredictability of nature's temporality, which, thankfully, is so good at disrupting the somber continuity of spatial proportion that maps usually force onto us.

The inclusion of cherry trees on the maps emphasizes what helps us get by instead of what helps us get around. It reminds us, when noticed, that for a couple weeks of the year, Tokyoites love to turn away from the ordered angles of mapped-out, boxed-in lives to walk and sit by flowers, with friends, colleagues, and family.

How I Ended Up Here

"Why did you come to Japan?" is a strange question, but one I get asked all the time. My friends and family can't understand it and my students and colleagues can't understand it. I'm not sure I understand it. Many foreigners who live in Tokyo have all kinds of great reasons. They came looking for opportunity, excitement, knowledge, money or love. They arrived in this country as students, lovers, company employees, job seekers, travelers, Zen initiates, pottery apprentices or other roles.

I am always impressed with those kinds of people and their serious, earnest reasons, but I really came to Tokyo as more of a lark. I thought it would be interesting. It has been.

Few people have such luck to live comfortably in another country, and if people had the choice to do what I do, live in another city and teach their home culture, they probably would. Travel, immigration and expatriate life is incredibly common in the world. We tend to think that countries are made up of homogeneous cultures and people who all look alike and live alike, but that's not true anymore, if it ever was. This historical moment in the world is filled with people like me living and working in other countries.

This question about why I live here is a variation of what I call "the food conversation." This is a common exchange I have with Japanese people who quiz me on what I like to eat and what I don't like to eat. Do I like *natto*? *Shiokara*? Can I use chopsticks? Even Japanese who have lived overseas for many years ask me whether I can adapt to the food here. Of course, one can easily live in Tokyo without ever eating any Japanese food whatsoever. Cuisines from all over the world could easily fill up the menu of any Tokyoite.

And yes, for the record, I love Japanese food, sake, raw fish, even *natto* is not so bad, though I can't say that I usually buy it at the grocery store as part of my regular purchases. I can use chopsticks. I don't like *shiokara*. A lot of Japanese, I've discovered, don't like *shiokara* either. *Bentos* are fine but kind of small and the fish sometimes boney. *Nihonshu* is fantastic.

I realized finally that "the food conversation" is really asking me why I stay in Japan, how I live here, and can I adapt to it. Those questions seem very Japanese. Americans would rarely ask that question to someone in America. I think that sometimes I'm being asked to hear a compliment, how great Tokyo is, or to hear some complaint, how expensive and crowded it is. Maybe also Japanese

How I Ended Up Here

feel they fit their world here because they are Japanese. Japanese-ness, whatever that means, is a way of adapting and surviving here.

Most foreigners who come to Japan find their niche and live reasonably comfortably, but never much get into the culture. Other foreigners seem to entirely throw off their native skin and become extremely involved in the life here. I suppose I am somewhere in between. I haven't quite adapted to a lot of aspects of life here, and I complain about all the hassles sometimes, too. But in that, I'm no different to the majority of Japanese living here. Tokyoites love to complain, often when they are most enjoying themselves. For me, it has been strange, frightening and exciting to go to a place where I knew basically no one and nothing, had no job and then figured things out. But for me, that figuring out means more than practicalities like food. It is about figuring out what life here means.

Tokyo contains an un-Japanese flavor that makes it a world city where anyone might live comfortably, though that is often ignored or concealed. Many Tokyoites live lives not so different from people in New York or London or Singapore or Hong Kong. Tokyo is a lot more western city in a lot of ways than people admit. Things like art, music, culture, restaurants, and stores, basically everything from around the world is here somewhere. Tokyo is a kind of global cultural museum, though the various rooms of that museum are disconnected and hard to locate.

I live in a way at times that has become very Japanese, and at other times fiercely hold on to my American-ness or western-ness. I vacation in Japan and vacation abroad. However, that is the same as most Tokyoites, who increasingly incorporate foreign languages, cultures, lifestyles and people into their way of living. When I look around an Italian or French restaurant, I see plenty of people eating, drinking and enjoying the evening in the grip of another culture. Other people tend to look at me when I'm enjoying the grip of Japanese culture in a traditional *izakaya* or *sake* bar. We're coming to the other culture from different directions, but we're coming to it.

At my university, Meiji Gakuin, I teach American literature, film, and art, as well as intercultural communication. Students' English level is high enough I can work with them almost entirely in English. The students are interesting and interested, and in the process of learning, they bring Japanese culture to me as part of their comparative way of learning my culture and language. Giving a lecture on Jackson Pollock and then passing through Shinjuku on the way home naturally sets up contrasts and counterpoised ideas in my mind. Writing about Tokyo helps me explain more clearly, understand more deeply and interact with greater sensitivity.

I live here too because I like to write. I started writing

about jazz on an online magazine, which led to writing in the newspaper, which led to editing a bilingual jazz magazine, Jazznin. I always loved jazz, so when I found the thriving jazz scene in Tokyo, I felt right at home. Jazz is a uniquely difficult music to play, and to write about, because of its emphasis on improvisation and intricate structures. So, that a dozen great jazz clubs have music every night makes it easy to enjoy any evening out. Writing about jazz just makes it all the greater pleasure.

Writing about why you live where you do can bring up a lot of anxiety, confusion and doubt. Have I made the right choice? Would I not have been happier in Beijing, or Paris or in my hometown? "Why did I come to Tokyo?" and "Why do I keep living here?" are questions I ask myself all the time. I am not sure these essays answer those questions, but to some degree they do. I realize that maybe I came here to write these essays, though I never knew that until I was writing them.

Part Two

A Beautiful Confusion

Frames of Emptiness

Atomic molecules are said to be mostly empty space and Tokyo, surprisingly, is not so different. Though one of the most densely populated and architecturally packed places on earth, Tokyo's buildings, homes and structures distance themselves from each other with dividing gaps. Of course, large cities all over the world have alleys, lots, and cut-out areas, but Tokyo's gaps are another kind of open space altogether. Calculating the combined area of these gaps, an incredible total of Tokyo's highly expensive land lies unused.

In New York, bricks cement buildings together fully and in Paris, London or Vienna, the stone fronts of row houses can extend the entire length of boulevards without a single gap. The piece-meal nature of Tokyo could have no stronger proof, but gaps are not just leftover scraps of space. These gaps are vital to the architectural feel and function of Tokyo, a necessary pause in the imposing conglomeration of millions of buildings.

These gaps vary in size, with gates, doors, fences and half-walls blocking the entrances. Most are so narrow hardly a cat can get through while others thrust up dizzying dozens of floors. Even some of the hand width ones have a door, though I can't imagine why. They're smaller than most closets. Some few have been remodeled with brick, tile or rocks, like mini urban *kare-sansui* rock gardens. The vast majority, though, are just about right to jam in a bicycle, hold an air con unit or rest a broom and dustpan.

Ironically, though, in a country with the best-swept gutters in the world, where neighbors spend as much time neatening their trash as reading the morning paper, these gaps are piled with tossed-out crap. Broken household appliances waiting for recycle coupons, buckets and mops leftover from *osoji* spring cleaning, unused kerosene containers, and ripped-out PVC piping all lie amid some of the world's toughest, most adaptive urban weeds. The gaps are the shameful backside of the proud, clean fronts.

Ranging up inside the gaps, air conditioning units array themselves neatly on newer buildings and chaotically on older ones. Well-taped air conditioning lines, television cables and thickly insulated water pipes hang like inorganic jungle vines. When wide enough, laundry flaps and futons flop on teensy drying poles. Dust, grime and dirt accumulate as they do in the attics or basements of American homes. It's a little embarrassing to think of all the stuff back there, as if there should be a place inside for all that, though of course in Tokyo, there is not.

Frames of Emptiness

Often behind stores or restaurants a door opens up onto plastic cases and storage cans. In back of restaurants, stacks of cabbage, soaking bean sprouts, and boxes of supplies spill out and you can see men in white aprons and rubber boots washing cabbage, cutting onions or taking a smoke break. At night, the gaps turn into cat heaven— the perfect space for Tokyo's feline population to prowl, mate, shit and give birth with cat-screams that echo piercingly between the two walls on either side. Without gaps, cats would have a tough life in Tokyo.

Not only for cats, these gaps offer essential psychological space. When I moved into a small house in a neighborhood so crowded I could reach out the window and touch the house next to ours, the distance seemed frighteningly close. But, I came to realize, it was still distance. I could hear the neighbors brushing their teeth, yet, there was a small cinder-block wall, a metal gate and enough room to toss out old futons on either side. Even that little distance seemed a luxury.

Every city's cultural awareness of personal space is different and being polite means entering into that awareness. The gaps around buildings feel at times like a cultural "building code." Of course, gaps provide ventilation and fire prevention, but rely on a respect for territory. As golf courses are the ultimate expression of power, gaps express a moderate amount of power. Regardless of le-

Beauty and Chaos

gal restrictions detailing how close buildings can be built, these gaps proudly display one of Tokyo's most precious commodities—space.

The gaps function like the space people leave between themselves when they bow. They know they will bow, so arrange themselves at the right distance to avoid smacking heads. Buildings don't bow, except in fanciful anime films perhaps, but they do give room to let in a shaft of light and a whisper of wind. Without that, Tokyo would feel too dense, like a rush hour of buildings. Inside most homes, space is divided by sliding doors. Outside, Tokyo divides solidity with open space. The gaps work like inverse *shoji*, using air to divide spaces instead of paper.

Few areas of Tokyo have architectural coherence like in the west, where entire sections of cities were built at the same time. Instead, one building stands up at one time, divided by a gap from another building time altogether. Tokyo's patchwork quilt is thus sewn together not with cement or mortar, but with open space. The gaps form a frame of emptiness around otherwise imposing buildings and lend a kind of fragility to the entire urban layout, as if the city is a row of dominos waiting to be tapped to have each knock over the next in a long flowing line of energy. The gaps though, too, soak up excess structural energy to give a reprieve from Tokyo's intensity.

Most strikingly, the gaps create an atmosphere of loneliness, as if all the buildings stand apart from each other like strangers without communicating too well. As I pass by them, they feel like a blink of sadness, a glimpse at the inner mind of Tokyo's architectural face. These gaps form a kind of structural "*ma*," like the pauses so important in Japanese conversations. The gaps let the city catch its breath and offer, amid the overpowering density of Tokyo, the relief of a moment of emptiness.

Clothing That Shouts–T-shirt Words

Fashion takes some strange turns in Tokyo, none more so than slogans on T-shirts. The impulse to wrap oneself, or more specifically one's chest, in words, usually English words, is a genuine source of summertime humor and insight. Anyone with a *fureeta* part-timer's income can catch a passing eye and make a surprising statement. To me, these post-modern slaps in the face are a welcome invigoration to the generally mundane shirts. T-shirts with slogans poke ideas and sentiments at Tokyoites content with non-confrontational appearance. Instead of style, they offer thought.

Excluding T-shirts that advertise brand names, sports teams, concert tours and obscure events, the best T-shirt writing produces a pause for serious consideration. Like a Zen *koan*, they subvert rational thought, provoke in-sight and come loaded with meanings. The very best are potent reminders of powerful ideas and profound senti-ments. Others are whimsical sound bites of aggression, lashes of disaffection, clever insight, and expressions of that studied nonchalance that young Tokyoites affect so intently.

Beauty and Chaos

Though public English in Japan is often derided for its incorrect grammar and foolish phrasing, these T-shirt slogans lately are all correct—indeed VERY correct. Here is a roundup of my favorites, all really seen by me and hastily scrawled into my notebook after I glimpsed them on streets, trains and shops around Tokyo the past couple summers.

Many T-shirts have narratives that suggest little stories. "Two years ago…" and "Special thanks to…" let you finish the sentence or wonder at the blank. Others sketch an instant situation in a clear tone of voice: "You're fired!" has all the anger of idiotic bosses everywhere, while "just you wait" is inflected with the finger-wagging bitterness of anyone seeking revenge.

"The effect was magical" makes you wonder, the effect of *what*? "The moment of supreme bliss" is *when*? "Just did it" over a Nike check mark is a nice bit of anti-advertising (like "MICROSHIT" in imitation Microsoft lettering), and makes you wonder, did *what exactly*? The longer, "If there's anything I can do to help, just let me know" promotes a kind of false concern and ironic redirection of your inner narrative that is especially comic during the madness of a hot commute.

Self-referential statements of identity seem to hardly need articulation but capture common and romantic stereotypes. The simple "songwriter" and "copycat" get

Clothing That Shouts—T-shirt Words

right to the point, while "fashion victim" ought to be handed out at Harajuku station free. "EMPLOYEE ONLY" and "substitute" contain a self-excusing clarity. "I'm not just a pretty face" feels like an apologetic pick-up line while "Too good to be true" sounds like maybe not ironic self-praise, though assertiveness is essential to a strong T-shirt effect.

On young, well-dressed girls, carefully capitalized T-shirts with "ROCKIES," "BOUNTY" and "PEARLY GATES" left little to the metaphorical imagination, and drew my gaze right to their breasts faster than any push-up bra. Maybe that's the point, or perhaps just the opposite, a kind of open criticism of the stares men give women. Even more suggestive on women were "everything in the garden's lovely," "good news for your hot party," and the even more provocative "BOY SCOUT RALLY."

Men, too, offer seductive markers on their fronts: "Independent Trick" and "high performance" both clearly offer sexual innuendo and self-bragging. These T-shirts seem less camouflage than mating call. Others, though, like "naked in blue" offer comic bewilderment. The absurd illogicality works like the punch line of a joke whose beginning you didn't hear. *Sodai gomi*, one of the few T-shirts in Japanese, clearly joked about men's tendencies toward sloth with its meaning of "Big Trash."

Other T-shirts seem to appropriately fit the wearer. Together with a floppy cotton bag, long braided hair, and ethnic print skirt, "additional parts inside" fit well the earthy style of one young woman in Shimokitazawa. Likewise, "I'm very pleased about it" on a platform-heeled, deeply tanned, dyed-hair Shibuya *center-gai* girl needed a second re-reading after taking in the whole package, but fit. Her friend had "GARU," which I assumed was either the verb ending "to want" or a *katakana* misspelling of "girl." Or both.

It's not all sexual suggestion and body consciousness, though. Ideological battles are waged on these individual walking billboards as well. The 60s idealism in the exhortatory "PROTEST AND SURVIVE" and the cosmic-minded "I am you, You are me, We are they" squares off against the nihilism of "sick of it all" and "shoot the suits." Of course, just wearing a T-shirt is a kind of suit shooting, and most Tokyoites wear "sick of it all" expressions on their face, if not in English on their shirts. "People look so much better alone" and "Sentenced to life on planet earth" comment on social alienation and the human condition. "Not sponsored," reminds that in this day of consumerism, almost everything is sponsored except individuals, though that may be next.

Command forms also present ideas and options. A couple favorites of mine, "don't stop" and "spread out" seemed to fit the rush hour perfectly. It's hard to read "quit

Clothing That Shouts—T-shirt Words

your job" and not mentally run through all the reasons why you can't actually quit your job. "Do not stack over 12" high", "post no bills", and "Keep back 200 Ft." steal familiar phrases from various situations and magically transform them into compelling statements about human relations. "Think WAHOO!" is a pleasant command for transcendence, with "Wahoo" being both a Japanese word and the English phrase one shouts when having a great time. It worked—reading it, I DID think "WAHOO!"

But, the ultimate test of efficiency and delicacy of expression is the one word T-shirt. Reduced to the smallest unit of meaningful exchange, these minimalist statements prove that less is more. "PLAY" beside a large arrow showing where to press makes an eloquent comment on the automatization of the human in this age of pre-recorded playback. In contrast, "analog" reminds how non-digital human nature remains. "CONFLICT" and "PROVOKE" both achieve their meanings. The simple "closed," which was not backed by an "open" on the other side of the T-shirt, revels in a suggestive, ambiguous simplicity.

Perhaps because they are in my language, I notice these words amid the bland school uniforms, grey business suits, and cheap discount outfits, but just the same, they form a unique and complex style of signification. The T-shirts seem a natural expression of the high literacy of Tokyo's populace, but reveal a sense of irony and fun that is all-

Beauty and Chaos

too-often hidden deep inside.

Catching these phrases is an art in itself. The vast majority of Tokyoites roll by without even a casual glance outside their blinders of visual indifference. Making a comment in English silently in written form is perhaps easier than actually making the argument in a direct conversation, but the meaning is powerful and affecting. As one T-shirt said most emphatically, "THIS AFFECTS YOU!"

Standing Libraries

Among the many *tachi-nani* of Tokyo, *tachi-gui* (eating), *tachi-nomi* (drinking), *tachi-uri* (peddling), *tachi-banashi* (talking), *tachi-mi* (looking), (an advertisement calls public pay showers, *tachi-onsen* or standing hot springs bath) the most compelling is *tachi-yomi*, standing reading. In a city that charges for space for every hidden, private pleasure, it seems an unusual public service to allow all that public reading for free. One wonders if the Ministry of Education secretly supports it as cheaper than increasing funding to libraries or reforming the schools. *Tachi-yomi* is mass education at its most "upright."

At any bookstore, convenience store, kiosk, or sidewalk pile of recycled oldies, long rows of well-pawed magazines are never without a row of people. They revolve gently as newcomers wiggle in, make a right-left survey of titles, and then ease into a close-kneed bend for a handful of pages on the thigh-high shelf. The bright lights above the racks are not coincidence, but courtesy—bathing the words as a public service—an illuminated invitation to cleanse the visual palette, to see clearly, to read standing up.

Beauty and Chaos

All along the row of standing readers, bags, briefcases, and backpacks dangle at bored angles. A college student drops his jam-packed schoolbag between his scruffy, oversized shoes, a high school girl slips her cell phone under her arm, a young salaryman loosens his tie, a well-dressed matron readjusts her department store umbrella on her forearm. The racks organize everyone into standing subsections—manga, guidebooks, bestsellers, politics, hobbies, fashion and fanzines. Every interest is accommodated, though the readers don't always fit their sections. Many people are clearly "cross-reading" what they wouldn't normally buy.

The etiquette of only choosing the already wrinkled copies on top and in front, then replacing them neatly in the right spot is rigorously maintained. After all, fresh, clean copies, for purchase, remain inviolate further back in the stack and underneath the rack. Everything from haiku to pro wrestling is treated with equal respect. If you want to buy something, you dig for a clean, un-read copy from the back.

Some standing readers lock their knees to finish an interesting snippet, frowning with attention, while others flip and shuffle, dissatisfied. Turning pages necessitates a full body adjustment, a quiver of taut muscles, a checking on the between-legs bag, a lazy smoothing of glossy paper, the inevitable finger licking to find a page more worthy of

Standing Libraries

attention. Always, though, standing readers lose themselves quickly and deeply into a text, before moving on the next.

People must stop to read for the blandest of reasons—waiting for trains or buses, not wanting to spend money, feeling embarrassed at purchasing slightly pornographic material, having no more shelf space at home, being sick of shopping, arriving too early, wanting to keep some friend waiting a little, trying to cut down on smoking, or being trapped by any number of other permutations of the complex linking up of times, people and places in a massive city where a slight lateness or earliness can amplify itself into a much larger period of time and an avalanche of apologies.

Yet, the fervent crowding at the well of words seems to be something more than just urban practicality. They can't all be not-doing something else. Tokyoites love to read, and love to read for free. Standing reading is an essential practice with a long history of public announcement boards and newspaper and magazine displays. One wonders at the economics of it all, with so many stores selling so many kinds of reading materials, but letting people stand and read feels as much public service as clever business ploy.

Some standing readers seem to have finished entire magazines, a series of articles, a cycle of manga stories, a rote memorization of movie schedules. They've gotten a choice of recommended restaurants, shopping venues, drinking places, a quickie soft porn climax, fashion remake tips, and reams of pointless, hip knowledge. They are standing reading for all the same reasons readers always read, only they do it a little more quickly.

More importantly, they seem to have managed an entire attitude transformation in just a page or two. Standing readers pick up more than casual info and save a few yen—they are stilling the fast pace of the city. As standing readers drift away into their next trajectories along the consumerist venues of shopping malls, streets, and stations, they seem refocused and returned to a calmer balance. They walk more slowly and more deliberately, clearly pondering over the meaning of what they read.

Standing reading effects a wonderful metamorphosis on book-loving Tokyoites, transforming them from gang-pressed zombie commuters into standing literati moving their minds amid a stillness of the body, instead of the other way around. Tokyo demands a lot of movement and filtering out of extraneous stimuli. Standing reading reverses that. Readers stop and focus.

By standing reading, the spiraling, unkempt threads of Tokyo's sensory assault can be stemmed for a few minutes and that always feels very, very good. Like all the best methods of recovery from frenetic daily motion, standing

Standing Libraries

reading is a directed recovery. It's a simple pleasure, and like all simple pleasures, it's therapeutic, and yet spiritual as well.

All over Tokyo, transfixed pillars of stoic humanity, readers stand with the wings of books spread out in a revolving vigil to keep alive the practice of the still contemplation of words.

Reading the Signs

In Tokyo, a sign has the power to make or break a business, to keep customers coming in, or turn the exterior face into a barrier. Japanese society is organized according to careful accountings of inside and outside. Houses, families, circles of friends, business relations, and indeed consciousness, all separate into *uchi* and *soto*, inside and outside, with signs in the middle.

In Tokyo, signs define the separating line between inside and outside and serve as a fulcrum for movement from one to the other. Yet, space is never so clearly divided as in the west. In Japan, *uchi* and *soto* is as much a conceptual difference as a physical one, but what are fascinating are the signs that negotiate movement from one space to the other. Tokyo is filled with these signs.

Reading the signs for stores, boutiques and especially for restaurants becomes an acquired skill. When I first came to Tokyo, I was not so good at it. A Japanese friend gave me a few practical pointers ("Never go into a shop with one elegant *kanji* on its sign, you can't afford it!" "Never eat at a *soba* place with dust on its display!"), and gradually, I learned how to manage unknown variables, fill in information, run through comparisons, and mentally thumb through guesses in order to understand signs.

Reading signs takes a great deal of experience and subtlety, like interpreting a poem. Often, I find that the smaller the store, the more difficult to interpret. The signs for larger stores, the department stores or chain stores, contain rather simple denotative meanings. Smaller places, though, rely more heavily on their signs with great attention paid to the color, font, carving, tone, texture, placement, wording and overall feel.

The signs capture in their specific form the character of the internal area. Each detail of the sign carries condensed meaning. I can understand why many Tokyoites do not trust their intuition, but read through magazines filled with recommendations, which are essentially, translations of the signs' complex, dense communications into other words.

For example, a chalkboard on a tattered easel outside a dark framed window is difficult to interpret, even with a solid set of sign reading techniques and intuitions. What can I make of this sign? I can see this restaurant serves some sort of African food, coffee, desserts and whiskey. I think back to a similar little place in Shibuya, and another a friend recommended, but looking at the sign, I cannot tell if it is authentic cuisine or just a bunch of *fureeta* faking it.

Reading the Signs

I could step inside and check it out, see if the food looks good from the décor, and soak in a bit of the interior, but often in this kind of situation, I walk on in search of a better sign.

Sometimes, I read the signs wrong. One sign written in old script on a dark black lacquer wood plaque offered the promise of a traditional Japanese place trying hard to serve up solid, Japanese food. However, the food was created on the modern idea of what traditional Japanese might be, not on actual tradition. The service was too formal, cold, distant, a place to impress someone but not to unwind. I thought back to the sign and could see it was all written there. The sign was not an old one, just made to look old. I read it wrong.

At another place, I understood the lively red characters surrounded by hiragana to be a more modern place, with the waiters and cooks relaxed enough to look you in the eye. I could ask what strange dishes contain and act a little drunk, even if you really are not. I got it right. At another place, though, I could see that the all-*romaji* sign was too easy to read and maybe not enough like real Italian. The dishes had plenty of sugar for younger consumers, and the interior was as brightly lit and superficial as the outside sign. The sign was too sweet and trying too hard. I wouldn't go back, but improved my sign-reading technique.

Beauty and Chaos

At the other extreme, some places do good business and are unconcerned with new sign-caught customers. One sake bar in Koenji had its long-time sign fall off, and instead of putting it back up, the master, who was a real connoisseur of sake and a gourmet of small dishes, just leaned the sign against the back wall beside the refrigerator. He just shrugged his shoulders and smiled when I asked why he had not put it back up outside. He was obviously beyond signs.

Of course, in every country signs outside to some extent show what's inside, but in Tokyo, the signs do even more than that. The signs act also as passwords, kind of magical "open sesame" words to create a dynamic conversion from outside to inside, from one way of thinking and feeling to another. Before even entering, the sign reader is already transformed into a participant in a way of dining, relaxing, drinking, ordering, and participating in the atmosphere of the place. The sign defines and indicates not only the food and atmosphere, but the entire experience of the reader turned entrant.

The sign helps create the right atmosphere, by marking the environment, and once inside, you are very distinctly playing your part: whether serious gourmand; brief slurper of noodles; lively bon vivant; or relaxing worker pleased for a solid belly full of food. I always feel very changed after entering places in Tokyo, and the sign points the direction of that change. I act a little more European in French restaurants and more Japanese in Japanese places.

The sign outside then has written on me as I pass underneath or beside it. It marks me and instills meanings in my behavior and feeling. These signs serve an essential regulatory and affecting function in Tokyo. And once back outside, the sign releases its hold on me and I walk away somehow back to myself.

The Point of Point Cards

My wallet has never been thicker than in Tokyo. It's thick not with money, but with point cards from every conceivable type of store: department stores, coffee shops, jazz clubs, foot massage clinics, electronic stores, a wine store, and even a specialty sock store. Whatever shop I go into seems to hand me another card. I jam it in among the other cards and wonder what the wallets of other people—people who actually want the cards—look like. They must be huge.

Like Tokyo, the cards remain eternally half-finished. I have only five more bagels to go before I get a free cookie, twenty more CDs before the 100-point mark (3,000 yen off), and two kilos of coffee to go before a hard-earned discount on the next purchase. Some places, like the foot massage, I've only been to once, but I still carry around their card hoping to some day receive another stamp in the foot massage "tour."

I feel exasperated carrying them around and yet irritated when I forget to get them stamped. If I forget to bring the right card, they just give me a new one, so I keep them all right inside my wallet. The paper fold-over cards battle for space with subway cards, credit cards, charge cards, and actual cash, replicating the chaos of Tokyo's urban layout. These little works-in-progress wait silently in my pocket, unfulfilled until the next round of stamps.

As I stand at the counter, I love to watch the clerks stamp these little cards with such seriousness of purpose. While counting the boxes, taking the store seal and carefully stamping the right number of accumulated points, I can tell the clerks are calculating how many more purchases will get me something free. "*Ganbatte!*" I hear them silently encouraging me, in that Japanese way. Secretly, I suspect, they are a little surprised that a non-Japanese, and a man, would be so attentive to what is, after all, an incredibly small issue in the grand scheme of life. They want me to share that particular Japanese delight in the miniscule.

Other consumers clearly pay close attention. My local shopping area has a system called "merit" shopping. Like at grade school, I rack up gold stars for good behavior, or in this case, little pink flowers to trade in at the local mom-and-pop shops. A tofu purchase lessens the price of a light bulb, which adds up in pink flowers for a free pack of toilet paper or an extra beer. It's all rather confusing, even with the pink banners flying outside the designated "merit shopping" stores. I notice the savvy shoppers counting up their pink flowers carefully and realize I'm not really a re-

The Point of Point Cards

turn customer in my heart. This traditional Japanese virtue of frugality just tires me out.

I do like the feeling of being brought inside these store's inner circles, though. The cards mark my membership inside a group, an essential position in Japanese society, and take away that nagging feeling of being a stranger. They "want" me back! The stamped boxes show the history of our relationship, progressing together point by point. And though the shopkeepers usually fill in the cards in polite silence, the exchange becomes another ritual way of thanking customers. The card softens the otherwise unfeeling relationship of monetary exchange. It also turns the purchase into the equivalent of slow food, another round of back and forth, another thing to consider.

There is something ancient and official, too, in all this stamping, folding over of paper and minute accounting. The careful inking, handling and returning of the card create a major project out of what really is just a quick exchange. It always affects me, the seriousness of this traditional monetary ritual, demanding my signature and phone number. Could there be a black market in point cards, like for tickets or phone cards? I always feel I must carefully receive the point card with both hands, place it securely in the correct spot in my wallet and offer my thanks, while the clerk watches.

Of course, all this point card business has great practicality. These cards are designed to keep me coming back, but I tend to have them for places that I would return to anyway. Still, they serve as reminders, a paper "*irrashaimase*," inside my bulging wallet. Of course, the stores could simply lower their prices, but maybe that's not nearly as much fun as fooling around with all these little cards. I feel like a child going from train station to train station, or temple to temple, filling in a stamp library (or stamp rally?) on a holiday.

And once I finish a card, the clerks stand beaming, proud of my accomplishment. They compliment me as if I've won the lottery, before energetically drawing a finished mark on the card, attaching name and date as certification, and carefully making up a brand-new card to be filled up again. When that happens, it's like karma, and I realize there's simply no escape from the eternal cycle of points.

The Noisiest Time of Year

At the end of every year, Tokyo dresses up in its annual Christmas outfit. The fake colored tinsel, reindeer light sculptures, corny holiday songs, and singing plastic Santa dolls make Tokyo look much like American cities, at least on the outside. But what runs like a secret underground river beneath Tokyo's Christmas pretence are *bonenkai* parties—those unique and unavoidable spectacles of year-end release and relief.

American holidays have year-end parties, of course, but they tend to be smaller affairs, in homes or even, notoriously, in the working office itself. One December evening after work, colleagues throw decorations around the office and enact the ritual of the office Christmas party, complete with the timeless images of the drunken lampshade on the head and flirting over the copy machine.

Home parties are generally tedious and constrained, with family members and close friends gathering for too-sweet deserts, eggnog, and presents—always presents. Careful wrapping, clever choices, and comic cards enliven the evenings, but just barely. Large meals of turkey, with special holiday foods, take place mainly among families, making television sports and holiday specials an often very welcome diversion.

American Christmas parties are nothing on the scale of *bonenkai*. *Bonenkai*, or rather, *bonenkai season*, runs for the entire month of December. The raucous atmosphere of *bonenkai* parties finds co-workers, old friends, friends of friends, and acquaintances from interwoven networks jammed together into never-the-right-number of seats at restaurants throughout the city. Drinking, eating and talking are all carried on at double their normal levels. Some restaurants, like retail stores in America, must make half the year's income in one month. Americans buy presents; Japanese pay *nomiya* tabs.

Of course, the year's social rules are reconfigured in both countries, but more so in Japan. During *bonenkai* season, everyone in Tokyo suddenly relaxes. Something like Mardi Gras, *bonenkai* is a collective social catharsis, a huge indoor hanami party. The typical Christmas lead-up in America, however, finds children, and adults, on better behavior. Otherwise, they will get no presents. *Bonenkai* season unstrings the taut pressures of the year.

Loosening up, though, can be overdone. Most of the year, most Japanese wear public faces like Supreme Court judges, but at *bonenkai* season, they bend over the side of platforms and freely vomit. No one much seems to mind. In fact, it's expected, and taken with distant, if bemused,

The Noisiest Time of Year

toleration. But while the ability to ignore nasty drunks is a basic survival skill in Tokyo, I always feel like many people drink in order to try to get from others at least some of what they find hard to give themselves—tolerance and forgiveness.

Like the flu, *bonenkai* spirit spreads through the city. Japan, perhaps the quietest nation on earth, becomes roaringly loud. Restaurants are deafening. People leap out of their seats, shouting, laughing, carousing, and making more noise than they have all year, as if there were a budget of noise, like for road repair, that if not spent, would be lost.

Groups of friends and co-workers stand around on the street, arguing volubly about the *nijikai* next place to drink. Even in the cold, coats, ties, and jackets hang open at odd angles. Women rock on their high heels, hair askew. The trains, smelling like breweries from the collective, exhaled alcohol, become punk rock mosh pits. People jump on trains late—unapologetically late—and then lurch and bounce around like overstuffed, red-faced Santa dolls.

Most shocking, people touch each other. No matter how long I live in Japan, I can never get used to the general lack of hugging, kissing or even just touching in public. But suddenly in December, everyone is holding each other's elbows, throwing their arms over shoulders, and leaning in close, as if the relationship maintained

73

Beauty and Chaos

throughout the year has to be somehow physically reconfirmed. Sloppy hugs from distant relatives are one of the inevitabilities of American holidays, so I like seeing that similar need here.

Ultimately, though, this collective onslaught of relaxation seems a form of resignation; the year is over, it's too late to go back and change things, so accept it and get ready to move on. It is a kind of fatalism, which I never feel in American holidays, though seasonal sadness hangs in the air there as well. After all, the year's accumulated disappointments, failures and tragedies cannot be entirely washed away in a river of alcohol. Not everything is forgotten, nor can it be. Like holiday decorations, excessive exuberance covers up the pressures and melancholy of the year, but only temporarily.

I always ask myself whether *bonenkai* season is the true nature of Tokyoites? Or is the other eleven months really the essential character of the city? Christmas in America seems always an aberration from the norm. Before I can figure it out, though, the collective hangover of the ultra-quiet New Year, when one can barely find an open restaurant, always brings the season to a sharp, sudden halt.

Ordered Around–Public Rules

I hate being ordered around. So, it's surprising I've ended up in a city covered in orders, legal regulations, "friendly" advice, guidelines, patronizing explanations and endless lists of rules. Every public space in Tokyo is marked by dos and don'ts hung on walls, glued on windows and plastered across empty spaces.

There is virtually no escape. Walking around Tokyo involves a constant stream of orders about all aspects of public life: using trains, lining up, standing behind yellow lines, getting on and off escalators, parking bikes, following arrows through gates and even, amazingly, urinating. Over many station urinals hang small one-sentence signs admonishing the user to please take one step closer, so as, presumably, not to drip on the floor. Even that one momentary relief is not free from command.

Of course, most people never read those rules. Many are no more than figures with circled slashes. Some are too small to notice; others are clearly absurd. I would probably never have noticed them except for one puzzling poster that caught my attention. Staring through the humidity of rainy season, I saw a poster explaining correct umbrella usage.

I couldn't figure it out at first. My list of world problems does not include umbrellas, but apparently, three great umbrella abuses need general correction in Tokyo. The umbrella poster showed a rude man oblivious of poking out the eyes of people behind him on the stairs, insensitive to dripping water and ruining others' shoes, and uncaring about knocking an old lady down the stairs when opening up his umbrella.

This set of umbrella rules struck me as so ridiculous that I began noticing all the others. Sitting down on the Inokashira Line, I could see I was surrounded. There were signs for headphones, priority seats, sticking one's fingers in the door and cell phones. Who thinks these things up? I wondered, but that was just the beginning.

I began to see rules everywhere. My bicycle parking lot had a twenty-item set of regulations bolted to the fence. Above the neighborhood trash collection point hangs a complex list of trash rules. I've never read the whole thing. The natural serenity of the public park down the hill from me is disturbed by official regulations about dogs, cooking, ball games, trash, smoking, skateboarding, in short, everything people go there to do.

The writers of these rules often try to lighten the tone through the use of cute manga. On most warning posters, exaggerated gestures or cutesy poses help deliver demands

Ordered Around—Public Rules

about everything from filing taxes to avoiding AIDS, refusing drugs, carrying guns, and voting, which was bizarrely compared to supporting a sports team.

The cutesy "Hello Kitty" getting her finger caught in the train door hardly reduces the authoritarian tone, however, or the farce. The common platform poster of a commuter racing onto the train shows his painful grimace when caught in the door and exploding stars when he falls. Instead of sparing embarrassment, these caricatured commands re-create the rules as slapstick. They submerge the violence to let us laugh, but still dictate behavior.

All this scolding feels like having the meanest grade school teacher imaginable following you all over the city shouting "*Dame!*" There's a connection, too, to that favored command of Japanese mothers, "*Abunai yo!*" "That's dangerous," converted, just slightly, into adult form.

These signs are well intentioned, I suppose, and ultimately, maybe needed. Despite the general orderliness of Tokyoites, corralling hordes of people into acceptable behavior is no easy task. Relative to other cities, though, Tokyo is amazingly ordered. So, which came first, the strict rules or the basically good behavior?

The signs control and contain annoying and even dangerous behavior, but also reveal that rule breaking must be going on all the time. No one could read all those signs; and even if they did, they could hardly think about them;

and even if they read and thought about them, it's doubtful they would change their behavior as a result. The man running to leap on the train will not stop mid-flight. The rude girl shouting into her cell phone is not looking around at warning signs.

Still, for me, that push and pull between breaking rules, which the anonymity of the city allows, and controlling actions, which is necessary for everything to function amid such human density, forms one of the most interesting tensions of the city. When will the next violation occur? I always wonder. And then, unexpectedly, it always does.

But, perhaps Tokyo functions through an awareness of others. One large train poster about cell phones pictured a huge cell phone screen with the mail message, "You're bothering the people around you." This embedded sign within a sign captured that special aspect of Tokyo culture, a getting out of the way. And maybe, ultimately, that's all that can be expected.

The Delicate Ritual of Small Change

After returning from abroad, I always stumble over my first few purchases in Tokyo. I tend to sling the bills around like a cowboy at a whiskey bar. In America, Europe or Asia, slapping money on counters, bar tops or tables offers a rather satisfying sound—coins clink loudly, paper lands with a noticeable thud—but in Japan, money is handled with silent ease, accompanied only by the soft murmuring of thanks. It always takes me a few startled clerks to remember my money manners again after returning.

Every time I buy something in Japan, I am amazed at the way money is passed back and forth with such delicacy. This complex and cordial ritual of exchange, so easy to overlook, always brings the hustle-bustle of Tokyo to a momentary halt. The care in returning money renews my sensitivity about human interaction and reminds me of the value of even small change. More than most cultural sentiments thrust into the marketplace, polite handling of money has preserved a special significance here.

The interlocking series of small actions varies considerably of course from place to place. At my local grocery store, one checkout woman hands back my change in a carefully stacked pyramid. Like a magician, she quickly and neatly arranges the bank notes and sandwiches the receipt beneath the stack of coins. Leaning forward, she holds this out with both hands like a miniature suspension bridge. In return, I have to use two hands to receive it, before fumbling it into my pockets as she offers a crisp bow.

Of course, the mom and pop fruit stand is rather casual, but it is the casualness of family intimacy not an elaborate economic ceremony. Even there, though, small change is given its due respect, just as it is when friends settle up a bill outside a restaurant. It is always fascinating to see a group standing and neatly shuffling money back and forth between wallets to equally divide the cost. Afterwards, they bow, these friends and acquaintances, even to each other. A moment's crude accounting is softened and the relationship restored.

Most often, change is fanned out into a peacock pattern with coins dotting the top. Even young dyed-hair, multiple-pierced *fureeta* will take care to display the cash like a grade school origami project. At station kiosks, where perhaps the quickest exchanges of all take place, the women place my change firmly and precisely in the exact middle of my palm, like a handshake. They have to work fast, but are just as deliberately courteous.

The Delicate Ritual of Small Change

Most places, though, change is returned neatly and directly on round little trays. If I accidentally set my money on the counter instead, the clerk always quickly picks it up and sets it properly (with a hint of reprimand) in the tray. These round symbolic areas are like a miniature *genkan* entryway, letting the cash rest politely halfway while changing from inside to outside and, most importantly, keeping it ritually pure. Perhaps that is why money is nearly always handled by the outside door of restaurants; it is simply too unclean to deal with inside.

In Japan, money is a precious commodity but also very personal, something to be kept covered, not openly revealed. For special occasions such as weddings, funerals or holidays, money is secreted in elaborate envelopes. The cash is wrapped and buried deep inside layers and layers of folded paper, covered with elaborate calligraphy and bound with bright-colored strings and ornate bows. An exchange takes place, but discretely hidden away.

At most stores or restaurants, though, such veiling is not practical. That still point of existential tension when I am standing at the counter, the clerk is arranging the receipt, and the change is lying on the tray could always go embarrassingly wrong, so a formal ritual helps smooth it out. Of course, with the large-scale commercialization of chains and bigger stores recently, many clerks go through the motions with none of the feeling. Yet still, the body language of small gestures for handling money has remained almost as securely as the Japanese bow. Respect is essential.

These rituals keep massive numbers of people moving smoothly through the economic fabric, of course, but something spiritual lingers inside this ritual exchange. Like at a temple where the money quickly disappears into the depths of the thick wooden collection box, the actions of polite exchange remind us to be grateful, attentive and aware. Similarly, when change is given, a bow is made, and a moment's stillness offered, all is returned to a comfortable balance, as if even small change somehow partakes of the life force of the entire monetary system and deserves its own respect.

I am always reminded of this by the elderly woman at the liquor store near my station. Always smiling and chatting, she gives me my change more tenderly than anywhere else. Every time, she takes my hand in hers and places the change there, then folds my fingers tightly over it, as if I am a clumsy schoolchild still too young and foolish to comprehend the true value and meaning of money. And of course, she's right.

A Big Bowl of Japan

The time I truly and deeply feel most comfortable in Tokyo is bent over a steaming bowl of *ramen* noodles with chopsticks in one hand and spoon in the other. As I slurp noodles (several times a week), I always mull over all the metaphoric meanings, but typically, before I can get too deep, I'm eating and eating and then too full to think about it more. *Ramen* is a national obsession: soul food, comfort food and gourmet food all in one bowl. Shops are everywhere and long lines form at lunch. *Ramen* lovers plan their outings around favorite shops dotting the city. Books and magazines on *ramen* sell well.

Of course, *ramen* is originally from China, but now has become perhaps the most Japanese of eating experiences. Soba noodle restaurants are a close cousin, but always feel a little too tidy and prim, to me. *Ramen* present themselves straightforwardly without any pretentious extras like soba shop's well-wiped and traditional *noren* curtains. Few things in Tokyo are as gutsy and unconstrained as the mouthwatering view down into a warm round bowl of pure *ramen* pleasure.

Entering a *ramen* place always awes me, though I know

what to expect: multiple thick appetizing smells, a bustle of energy, the thud of my elbows on the thick counter, the off-balance, too-small stools, and always the steam. Once you enter, you become part of the total flow. First you get a ticket from the machine (saves the counterman dirtying his hands) or toss off an order. Two syllables suffice: speak the words "*shoyu*" and you'll soon have a bowl of soy sauce base, "*miso*" gets you a spicier, thicker soup, or just say "*ramen*" for the house specialty.

The number of choices can be complex: *kotteri* (oily), *asari* (light salt), thick noodles, thin, (or summery *tsukemen*), flavored egg, *menma*, and always something special to that shop. Most places, you have few choices and must accept the taste handed to you, and it's always better than what you would have picked. The best places, though, have their recipe down to just two choices, which are, inevitably, perfect.

Then wait patiently watching the preparations. Once they arrive, *ramen* are eaten without a break. It's basically one smooth, uninterrupted motion from the moment of nodding your head under the curtain to the *gochisosama* thank you on the way out. While waiting, you can consider the countertop choices: small bottles, chopsticks boxes, tissues (sometimes), water (always a relief to Americans), pepper, minced garlic, hot oil, special sauces, all offering potential modulations to get the taste just like you like it.

From the counter, I love to watch the graceful preparation that combines multiple techniques and patterns: first, lots of shouting, then, the easy slide of a handful of noodles into the boiling water, the initial preparation of the bowl, and the careful accounting of orders (none ever mistaken or lost). Between sips of water, I love to watch the slinging off of water with full *kendo*-like body strokes followed by the final delicate positioning—like an *ikebana* flower arrangement—of the bean sprouts, meat slice and seaweed. *Ramen* is a confluence of forces, big and small, into a perfect, round bowl.

The group feeling at *ramen* places contrasts sharply with fancy restaurants, with customers in small, separate groups, or other "quick" places where everyone remains isolated. At *ramen* places, you share everything along the counter: the water pitcher, the chopsticks, and the soy sauce container. It feels like a friendly gathering or a family reunion—a *ramen*-loving family. Nothing is ever said, but the feeling of camaraderie pervades the atmosphere. It always feels like everyone is eating from the same big pot.

And those common pots are gigantic, perhaps the biggest cooking utensil in a country where smaller is usually better. The pots for boiling water and heating broth are so massive they have to set up water spigots over the pots, rather than try to wrestle the full pots over to the spout and back again full. There is something ancient about those gigantic pots, like cooking for a huge festival crowd or an entire village.

But what I really like best about *ramen* is its unpretentious attitude. It's a welcome change from the foolishness of many restaurants. No one tries to drag you in, no one lines up fancy wine bottles and there is never a chalkboard of foreign language *katakana* outside. There are no discount tickets. *Ramen* is the comfort food of choice—good for a hangover and good for a holiday. If Japan can be said to be an orally fixated culture, then *ramen* is its most basic pacifier. There's no attitude, no pretence, no vertical hierarchy, everyone piles around the same counter on equally uncomfortable seats.

At a *ramen* shop, I feel Japanese really unwind, so I can too. Most other places have their own uptight annoyances and nervous impositions. At coffee shops, people worry and smoke. At *izakaya*, they overindulge and talk too loud. But with *ramen* everything is proportioned, balanced and hassle-free. Healthy and restorative, *ramen* are the *ofuro* bath of food—instead of outside, they bathe your insides.

In that sense, *ramen* is quintessentially Japanese, yet also rises to a universal level beyond the limits of any one culture's boundaries, where it satisfies a hunger—as social and cultural as it is physical. *Ramen* has touched the heart—and stomach—of this one non-Japanese, deeply.

A Big Bowl of Japan

Writing on most topics seems like a closing of sorts, but writing about *ramen* leads my mind out the door to a *ramen* shop to eat, and think, again.

Part Three
Scenes from the Train

The Paperback-Cellphone hypothesis

Tokyo resists all easy generalizations and hasty conclusions. Just when you think you've got a hold of a clear explanatory concept that you can sling around to impress people, you get an experiential slap in the face.

Here's one: I assumed that because the number of cellphones have increased, commuters would no longer read as much as they used to. Instead of soaking in great works of writing, or even pop bestsellers, they would spend their commuting time poking around on little pieces of plastic and silicone.

This hypothesis seemed obvious enough, all around Tokyo are stupid little jingles ringing, loud *moshi-moshi*'s, excited *ima doko desu-ka*'s all over the place. The *oyayubi-zoku* seemed to have reclaimed the mental input space. Newspapers, palm-size paperbacks, and magazines would surely lose sales as everyone spoke breathlessly into their little microphones and tapped out messages on their little input pads.

I feared that the highly literate culture of Tokyo

would have all its culture reduced to little screens, glowing buttons, and jagged, dancing text. Text messages just could never be the same as well-connected phrases, ordered events, conceptualized and explained ideas. Reading and written culture would retreat in the face of cellphone's dominance. The mind's sensitive, interior space would be disrupted and converted to absurd conversations. I felt certain that discombobulated, half-articulated speaking would establish an oral culture of immediate superficial answers and thoughtless chattiness—ALL because of cellphones.

Of course, I exaggerated too much. One Saturday night, I started looking around the train to see if my fears had any grounding. What I found was that reading was just as established as ever.

Saturday night, nine o'clock, Chuo Line: Nestled in the middle of the seven seated passengers along one bench was a new convert, her "KDDI" bag propped up as she gently poked around on her cellphone with the astonished face of novelty and promise. A black choker crossed the middle of her neck. OK, I was right. More cellphones were being sold every day.

But then to KDDI's left was a trim, proper woman in a white blouse and faded rose skirt, hose-covered legs set primly together. Her manner of calm poise spoke sophistication. Her starched collar angled out with boutique-

The Paperback-Cellphone hypothesis

bought care. Her hair was pulled back tightly, yet slipped provocatively out in one place from a large tortoise-shell barette. A demure, simple black leather bag rested in her lap, above which she balanced not a cellphone, but a paperback covered in a black leather book cover that matched her bag.

To her left was a plumpish young man in a yellow slogan T-shirt tucked inside a half-buttoned, well-washed cotton shirt, jeans-covered legs sprawling. Tousled hair complemented his half-tied Keds sneakers. He was not sending email on his cellphone, but poring over a largish NHK translation of a "Keiji (detective) Colombo" script. He obviously had his own ideas of the plotting of mysteries, the particular techniques of introducing clues and the revelation of motivational character. He was making notes in the margin. What he didn't have, though, was a cellphone.

To his left was a *ronin* type who shifted as uneasily as all adolescents do underneath a massive backpack crammed with study guides, history outlines, test tricks and review schedules. He was reading Young Jump magazine the whole time and certainly didn't reach inside for his cellphone. His friends might all be in university already, so he wasn't calling anyone. He was relaxing from a day of multiple-choice guesses by reading.

To the right of the KDDI poster girl still plunking away

on her new cellphone was an older woman, with grey hair resolutely un-dyed over an earthy cotton ensemble outfit. She was all wrapped up in an A4 size xeroxed copy of some journal article or other which needed annotation and comment from marks with her well-schooled pencil. Obviously, she wouldn't have a cellphone. She was just not the type.

Next to her was an OL in a short, tiger-print skirt. She had just taken some sort of class on cosmetics, the bag tucked neatly in her lap. Perhaps her date ended early, or perhaps she was just going to it. A simple paper-wrapped book consumed her attention, title concealed. No calls.

My theory of the cellphone's devastation of the reading culture looked in doubt. One more and I'd have to admit I was wrong. At the end of the bench, sat a woman in her 50s who held no alphabetical or ideographic writing, but the musical score from Franz Wullner's "Chorobungen." Instead of tapping the buttons on a cellphone, she tapped time on her leg, gently humming the melody—not a melody to use as a cellphone ring—to herself.

What amazes me most about Tokyoites reading on trains, after observing more of them, is how thoroughly they become lost in their books. The train is packed with stimulation and distraction, people, ads, clothing, passing stations, but most people fix their entire attention on the words on the page. Then, suddenly, they move from their

The Paperback-Cellphone hypothesis

position of calm, stoic focus just at their stop. Cellphone typing, in contrast, relies on jumpy, nervous motions. The thumb jumps around over the teensy pad, repeatedly jamming the keys.

Maybe that's what worries me most, to imagine a shift from placid contemplation of book ideas to the anxious oral messages of cellphones. Japanese, of course is really two languages—written and spoken. All languages have that divide, but the difference between the two is perhaps greater with Japanese. Written and oral become two ways of thinking and experiencing the world. The tension between those two modes manifests itself on Tokyo's trains, but the resolution is yet to arrive.

Still, it would seem that many people could answer the question "*Ima doko desuka?*" with "Right now, I'm lost in a book."

The Pumpkin Train–Late Night Commuting

Daytime commuting in Tokyo is the height of efficiency and convenience. But, at night, just past midnight, things reverse. The transportation system turns, like Cinderella's carriage, back into a pumpkin. Unlike the blithe convenience of daytime commuting, a trip home after midnight demands patience, money and savvy. One evening, I lingered too long and learned my nocturnal commuting lesson the hard way.

Whether you make the final, spectacular sprint for the last train or not, most trains leave by one a.m. In New York at one a.m., the second jazz set is just kicking up; in Paris, diners are finishing their cognac; and in Madrid, people are heading out to dance off their tapas. In Tokyo, though, at one a.m., things are winding down into inconvenience. Buses have already finished, about the same time as pachinko parlors. Lines for taxis stretch the length of unlighted stations. People act sullen and weary.

On the evening of my lesson, I set out towards home from a jazz club with a musician friend, late-ish but with plenty of time. Granted, I chatted too long at the door of the club, exchanged a few *meishi*, bought a bottle of water at a convenience store, and stopped at the station toilet, all the while talking to my friend about music.

Nonchalant high spirits should not be punished with the pumpkin treatment, but that's what I got. The usual 50 minute trip home turned into 170 minutes; an affordable 450 yen fare into a wallet-bleeding 8,000 yen.

My easy route would have been this: six minutes and 160 yen from Akasaka to Harajuku on the Chiyoda line; four minutes from Harajuku to Shinjuku on the Yamanote Line; and then the crowded but swift, 19-minute snoozer from Shinjuku to Musashi-sakai on the Chuo Line for 290 yen. From there, the taxi line can be a 15-minute wait, but it's only one click of the meter home. Leaving at 11:40, I should have had my teeth brushed and been asleep before one.

Of course, it didn't happen like that. That was still "normal commute" thinking. "Deep night" commuting rules soon took over.

My friend wanted to avoid squashing his guitar, fair enough, so we took the Chiyoda Line past Harajuku to connect to the, well, we were talking, true, and sort of went past, well, the station to change trains, the name of which, well, wasn't so clear exactly, it being over a year or so since he last went that exact route, but it wasn't even close to

The Pumpkin Train—Late Night Commuting

one o'clock, so why worry, right?

We got off one station past, turned around and headed back to Yoyogi-Uehara. That took five minutes train-ing, a few minutes up and down the stairs, and a fifteen-minute wait. We caught the 12:30 local back to Meidaimae, the last train, and then scampered down and under and up again to the right platform. There's always a smug contentment to being on the right train line platform. We felt very self-satisfied being in the right place and resumed our conversation. From there, it should have been a straight shot on the Inokashira Line to Kichijoji, where my friend lived. From there, I could make an easy transfer to the Chuo Line for two quick stops, then a brief wait for a taxi home.

Of course, it didn't happen like that. Let's just say we weren't so right as we thought.

The train was packed to guitar-smashing capacity. A lot of other people were equally inattentive, late and nonchalant. Like us, they were struggling from the "fun playing" areas of Tokyo to the "cheap living" areas. As it turns out, the last Inokashira Line stops four stations before Kichijoji. Since there is no room for all those trains overnight in Kichijoji, the last train parks far away, regardless of where passengers might want to go.

Had we known the train didn't make it all the way to Kichijoji, we would have taken the Meidaimae train we were previously on all the way to Shinjuku and then caught the Chuo Line from there. That would have at least had symmetrical regularity to it, making two 45-degree angles out and back for what would have been a straight shot from Harajuku on the Yamanote line. But of course, we didn't follow this illogical but infallible triangulation route.

Train fare total so far: 560 yen. Total time elapsed: 70 minutes.

What we also didn't know was that the reason almost everyone got off the train one stop before the last one was not because they lived there, but because that five-stops-before-Kichijoji station was located right near Inokashira Dori, a major thoroughfare where taxis pass on a regular basis.

Our four-stops-before-Kichijoji station was the kind of cute little wood-roofed station that you don't even see until you turn the corner, with a barely raised platform, no pedestrian overpass, and, needless to say, few taxis. We also should have followed the last little group of stragglers walking numbly towards better taxi hunting grounds, but we stood on the street by the station with pride, resolve and dwindling energy.

Thirty minutes and two trips to the convenience store later, a taxi, perhaps lost himself, arrived. We told him "Kichijoji" and he asked if we wanted to go along

The Pumpkin Train—Late Night Commuting

Inokashira Dori. We said, "Yes," foolishly, as it turned out. What he knew full well but we had yet to find out was that the street was under repair. "End of budget season," the driver told us smiling in the rear-view mirror. "Road repair funds must be spent. They work all night. Happens every year," he said with that formal pleasant manner that normally opens to conversation, but irritates when you are in a bad mood.

A normally zippy, no-traffic ten minute ride became a repeatedly braked forty-minute crawl past flags and blinking traffic barriers. 2,800 yen.

After alighting the taxi, saying good-bye to my friend and his guitar, I hustled towards the station with a rise of foolish optimism. I scarcely recognized it with the massive steel shutters yanked shut. The gates were sealed right on schedule, forty minutes before I got there. Encircling the station were two lines of people waiting for taxis, north and south. The patient, beleaguered taxi-waiters eyed me incuriously, looking as if they had been there since the station closed forty minutes earlier. I decided I would not stand there passively, but instead walk to a large intersection nearby, figuring I could flag a taxi there sooner.

But of course, it didn't happen like that.

The little red lights of the taxis shone "empty" in *kanji* as they shot obediently back to the taxi lines. Of course, the drivers respect orderly taxi lines, their very length at night must be a reassuring sign of good, solid income. A lone figure waving wildly in the middle of the street far from the lines must appear a symbol of mayhem, confusion and disruption. I waited about an hour.

The taxi driver who finally did pick me up usually worked out of Kabukicho. Maybe he thought a foreigner was more likely to be heading back there than anyone else; certainly he was a bit lost so far from his regular route. Anyway, whatever threat to social order I presented was no worry to him, since he was used to Kabukicho, forty minutes and a world away. And also, he had found a good chance to practice his English. That leg of the journey was unproblematic enough, but 2,600 yen nonetheless, with no English teaching discount.

Once out of the taxi, I walked the last five minutes comfortingly by foot. It was 2:30 when I got inside. I realized, as I brushed my teeth, it would have been easier, not to mention faster, to have just taken a taxi from right outside the club all the way back.

I realized why everyone's final dash for the last train is always so desperate.

Hanging On the Meaning

People in Tokyo hold themselves up in many ways. With as much variety and casual inattention as with everything else in this overgrown city, Tokyoites have perfected one essential, central survival skill—strap holding on crowded trains. The hand positions and body postures form an iconography as complex as any Buddhist statuary.

The standard hold is the "two-handed deliver-me-lord." Common as a sparrow, this interweaving of fingers around the plastic handle is of only passing interest to the specialist. The internal suffering is obvious, but the expressivity extends no farther than an occasional individualized flicking motion and predictable swaying. Still, it's the standard by which all others are measured. The thumbs often unfold to massage acupressure points between the eyes.

The other, more spectacular, two-handed hold is the "post-bacchanalian stabilizer." One hand on the anchoring cross bar and one hand on the strap allows for maximum weave, bounce, and windmilling. Particularly impressive at *bonenkai* season, adepts can twist up to 180 degrees. The more dangerous "double strap hang" allows for even greater degrees of rotation. Be very careful, though, of low-hanging, leaning-over poses. This can signal vomitus.

The "lovelorn arm-around" involves the entire body. The arm, often up to the shoulder, wraps around the vertical bars located, like frames for temple guardians, at either side of the doors. Outcroppings of various body parts, especially chest, belly, or hips, facilitate relaxing into a comfortable, bar-supported lean. Clasping hands around the bar is an alternative, while the full-body support allows for dreamy cell-phone re-checking and occasional sighing.

The "double-jointed open-palm hang" is an especially delicate and lovely hold. The long pull of the four straight fingers forms a perfect set of lines drawing the eyes up toward the ceiling advertisements pinned above like snapshots of heaven. The thumb, as if no longer opposable, tucks behind the finger-y tableau to add mystery to elegance. This hold is especially common among female commuters. Rings and bracelets are shown to maximum effect.

While on the issue of gender, the main distinction in technique between males and females of the commuting species is that women typically use fewer strap techniques because they simply have better balance. Even in high heels, they hold on less. Women who grip, however, make greater use of the adjoining tips of their fingers for a lighter, kneading pressure, while men tend to employ the full palm wrapped firmly around the entire handle or bar.

Hanging On the Meaning

The "caffeine tap" is an unceasing drum or roll of the fingers on the plastic handle often accompanied by humming or a bass line leaking from the earphones of the strap holder. Similar in youthful exuberance is the "fingernail display hold." The exterior cuticles, often painted magnificently, are framed by the handle, where they wiggle in the air for attention, frequently from the owner herself. The fingers often release the handle to allow for preening dyed hair and fiddling with accessories.

A cousin of the "caffeine tap," the "white knuckler" derives from unknown origins of tightly wrapped psychological intensity. All wrinkles, indeed all blood, are pushed out of the finger. Often the knucklebones seem ready to pop right out of the skin. This grip is often taut enough to remain entirely immobile for hours. Rare, but noteworthy is the "anti-bacterial cringe." This seasonal grip, most often seen in summer, involves a handkerchief, often light blue with flower patterns, which is wrapped around the handle. The hand is then placed on top of this protective cloth. The winter version simply employs gloves to shield the skin from viruses.

Of delicate demeanor is the "intellectual grasp." More common in the early morning hours, the fingers curl under the strap with the thumb in front, wedging a small pocketsize book just above eye level. Some readers of this book may even be using this technique right now as they read this sentence! Several variations for magazines and newspapers require advanced origami training, but the basics still apply.

Of special pathological interest is the "*chikan* re-channeling." This is basically an erotic massage of the strap. The hand rubs, fondles, twists, plucks, strokes and caresses the plastic handle in a series of close-eyed gestures. From time to time, the hand opens up wide and full with nostril-flaring release. After a moment of respite, the hand may then begin again squeezing gently. One can only guess what interior fantasies accompany this handhold.

The "silver bar, angular pull-up" is favored by those who may be among the fittest, but not among the tallest. Here, commuters in over-packed trains thrust an arm onto any metal bar they can grab. The angle of lean is the tricky part and must be adjusted and readjusted to maintain balance and backward pressure against the crowd. The exact trigonometric ratios between bar, arm, torso and knees of seated passengers can be intricate. The knees of beginners tend to whack the knees of sitting commuters, but this helps overall balance.

The "elbow pillow" is one of the most comic of commuting strap-holds. Masters focus on leaning fully and heavily into the little crook of the arm which nature provides as solution to fatigue, drink and boredom. The neck muscles loosen, while the hip and knee joints unlock at random, spasmodic intervals. With practice, though, anyone can learn to just drift right into deep-elbow REM sleep, staying half-conscious station after station, often to the end of the line. Drooling and tears are common additions.

Less comic is the "chain-gang manacle," which involves two steps: first, the hand goes through the handle past the wrist; then, the fingers ball up into a fist, locking the arm as firmly in place as any handcuff. While a rapid stop can twist the hand painfully, this hold clearly captures the imprisoning nature of commuting itself.

Many other techniques are worth study and contemplation, but the above form the basic set of meanings commuters convey in their complex mudra-like sign language.

The Ebb and Flow of Human Motion

I love to stand on the walkway overlooking Hachiko crossing in Shibuya and just watch the people move. The crossing has been captured in countless films, TV shows, news segments and ads. The masses of crossing pedestrians have become a symbol, of population density, urban isolation, Tokyo's vitality and human movement. The equivalent of entire cities pass through there every day. When I watch, and even more when I am whizzing through there myself, one question pops up again and again—Why doesn't everyone bump into each other?

Human motion in Tokyo is constant. There are people walking along neighborhood streets, to the bus stops, towards the station, around shops, pausing in front of kiosks, then up the stairs across platforms through stations and around and about the entire city. The movement of people in Tokyo never ceases, like blood circulating in a constant flow. And yet, with millions of people heading directly towards each other, they rarely smack into one another. It's amazing.

The quick, nimble motions that allow commuters to pass by one another with smoothness and gentleness are

Beauty and Chaos

a kind of marvel. The wiggling, hip jutting, shoulder twisting, bag adjusting and occasional stopping in place accumulate into a choreographed precision routine. This massive commuting dance is choreographed impeccably. A million people pass through Shinjuku station a day, yet collisions are few, even passing bumps are, percentage-wise, rare. Some "invisible hand" seems to guide everyone around everyone else accident-free.

Of course, I bump into people all the time. But I'm a foreigner, and even after years worming through crowds in Tokyo, I still haven't fully developed my body-avoidance radar as well as most Tokyoites. I occasionally step in the wrong direction, or get stuck bobbing back-and-forth from side-to-side with someone, or simply get trapped on the wrong side of a staircase, having to huddle down to wait for the disgorged trainload to pass by me before moving on. Still, I've improved.

When I walked through Tokyo crowds at first, I could hardly move. It seemed like every direction was blocked. Little by little, I found myself turning and responding in ways that have gradually become second nature. My body started to mimic those around me: turning my shoulders back to avoid a pair of older women, twisting to the right to avoid an oblivious couple, or speeding up to scoot in front of a cross cutting man. Double-quick steps, short pauses, scrunching up, squeezing through, and going the long way

The Ebb and Flow of Human Motion

around became movements as natural as breathing. My body adapted to Tokyo long before my mind did.

But, I'm still better than most "newbies." It is easy to pick out tourists new to Tokyo by the way they move. It is not just a stopping and trying to figure things out, staring uncomprehendingly at the unfamiliar space and strange motion. Tourists always come through crowds as if in their own bubble. When friends visit from abroad, they get so stuck and move so slowly I want to get a rope like for pre-school field trips, so they can keep up. Their bodies have not yet adapted to Tokyo. They dance another dance.

Of course, many Japanese are able to wade through a crowd with tremendous nonchalance and occasional unconcern. Tokyoites, too, get lost, move in one direction then randomly shift back, even stop outright before heading in the other direction. But they do it smoothly, even if with an embarrassed gesture at not following the right flow in the right direction.

In Tokyo, the flow of lots of people through little space is an ongoing conflict. Changes to improve the flow, though, don't always work as expected. The faster, smoother ticket machines and Suica cards have ordered the flow and sped it up considerably. However, when they fail, people slam into each other like tourists. Backing out of the ticket chute is one of the few times people in Tokyo really do bump into each other. The new escalators and elevators on train platforms result in waiting clumps of people, pushing into each other and moving in awkward ways. They have not yet learned the new motion through the new blockades.

Even with my acquired radar and evasive skills, I always feel I can't walk in Tokyo like I want to. If I speed up a bit or relax too much, I cannot move individually, but have to slip into various slipstreams of motion, like a school of fish all turning at the same time to avoid a predator or undersea obstruction. This moving with the group is not a natural mindset to westerners raised on the sanctity of personal choices and open spaces.

Cutting through the crowd with the stutter steps, side fakes and drawbacks of an NBA player can be tiring. Yet, at other times moving through this vast human flow feels exhilarating, like skiing through a forest or running in the lead pack of a marathon.

The motions, though, are perhaps more like dancing than any sport. Dance is perhaps the most unique form of cultural expression, special to each and every culture. No culture dances quite like another, since dance expresses the deepest layers of human motion and body rhythms.

Like an elaborate folk dance, certain set patterns and formal courtesies are always followed in Tokyo. Still, to me, that no one tramples anyone seems a daily miracle. And yet, more than that, Tokyo's puzzle of motion—huge

The Ebb and Flow of Human Motion

numbers of bodies moving through limited space—has an overwhelming kind of beauty, a beauty that combines all these human bodies flowing and moving in their own massive urban dance.

All the World's a Stage-Train Platforms

Shakespeare said "All the world's a stage," but in Tokyo, the grand human drama is acted out most often and seen most clearly in one single public place—train station platforms. Unlike café-lined European avenues or American super-sized sidewalks, Tokyo has few good people-watching spaces. Though crowds and closeness make it difficult, I prefer the unique, elevated stage of train station platforms. They are the best place to observe Tokyoites unselfconsciously acting out the drama of daily life.

In European train stations or American bus terminals, people tend to speed up towards their destinations or huddle together for last goodbyes. Tokyo's platforms, in contrast, are a place to catch one's breath from the forward thrust of city life. Tokyoites, so at ease with waiting on trains, reveal something, as they wait, of their true selves. Away from obligations, social roles and detailed schedules, Tokyoites' inner life emerges in small acts of human comedy and tragedy that you cannot see anywhere else.

April is especially open to performances, with so many

people taking on brand new roles. Parents bring their children to college, studying train maps to chart a new life journey. Freshers, first year employees in large companies, dressed in unwrinkled outfits and un-scuffed shoes huddle together in uneasy camaraderie, trying to decode company manuals and remember orientation lectures. Once, years ago, in late March, I saw a group of college graduates, all men, reeling drunk and weeping loudly. They had just graduated, apparently, and were hugging each other for the last time as one big group. Their goodbye was on the platform.

The uniquely complex social relations of Japan also appear vividly on platforms. Senior businessmen stand erect facing the train or striding towards the stairs, their juniors turned deferentially sideways. Nowhere else have I seen such precise and elegant bowing. The 90-degree bend of the body for relatives, older *senpai*, section chief *shacho* and clients turns the platform into a ceremonial site of elegant ritual. Every night, the platform becomes a kind of final stop, what Japanese call the *nijikai*, where last jokes and drunken ramblings round off the last of the evening's pleasures. There's no curtain fall, but the party isn't finally over until the train pulls away from the platform.

Vanity takes its turn as well. Platforms function as fashion walkways for young people to strut their newest costumes. The platform-turned-catwalk gives

All the World's a Stage-Train Platforms

them a place show off the latest outfit from the hippest magazines, all planned and put on as carefully as any actor or actress. Platforms always have mirrors and shiny surfaces seemingly to help these people reconfirm the perfection of their appearance. Their self-conscious displays work well as they walk past quickly glancing admirers.

Lovers, too, use the platform for the public part of their wooing. With pained, suffering eyes, they reluctantly separate, stoically accepting the parting of trains for opposite sides of the city. Tokyoites can live up to several hours away in different directions, so the platform might be the last lover's touch for days and days. Often, I see a couple holding hands and walking as slowly as possible along a platform, before deciding NOT to get on the train. Unable to part, they snatch a few minutes more in each other's company. I wonder how many confessions, proposals and admissions have been spoken on platforms.

Not all goes smoothly, though. One afternoon I saw a young man on his knees, bag thrown aside, hugging his girlfriend's knees. Her face was scrunched into a ball, tears barely stifled, as he begged her, for what, I couldn't hear. I watched their melodrama as I rode away up the escalator. Another day, a man who boarded the train right beside me left a woman standing on the platform with obvious heartache. Halfway to the next station, he reached in his pocket, pulled out a wedding ring and slipped it back on his finger, the day's deception complete.

Stupidity reveals itself just as often as the eternal verities of the heart. The shamefulness of acting like an idiot seems no inhibition on train platforms. Platforms are the only place I've ever seen a public fight in Tokyo. The pressure of work, drinking and overcrowded cars blows out onto the platform into a scuffle that ends only when passersby or a platform guard descends on the two combatants and pulls them apart. More often, late-night drunks crash out across platform chairs, sleeping in awkward positions, unable to manage any more. In America, they'd be robbed right down to their underwear.

Suffering, too, is present. One morning, I saw a mother, her face in her arms, weeping uncontrollably, her long hair soaked with tears. Her son, five or six years old, sat beside her, one hand on her shoulder, unsure of how to console her. No one stopped, and neither did I. Another day, people slowed and pooled around a trolley, which, on getting closer, I realized was a dead body being wheeled away. Someone had died on the platform and the ambulance crew was pushing the body-laden trolley towards the exit. Irritation at being slowed down quickly turned to a shudder.

Such adrenaline-charged situations are rare, though. Typically, platforms most often offer space for solitude. Like Giacometti statues, thin and crinkly, surrounded by vast open space, the platforms are filled with people standing utterly alone. The occasional crowd around them makes no difference, they are framed by a huge open area that creates an anonymity and loneliness like no other place in the city.

In Tokyo's frenetic rush, one can only be audience to these kinds of short mini-dramas; there isn't time for complete acts. The brevity, though, is part of the beauty and part of the impact. Though cell phones have started to soak up their share of human emotions and dialogue—at times the platforms seem like one gigantic phone booth—the sheer numbers of Tokyoites parading along and waiting patiently will ensure that this platform theater continues.

For me, platforms are always a chance to re-humanize in what is a very alienating city, even if only for the few short minutes before the bell and the whoosh of the train shatters the performance and signals the end of another play.

Slideshow Lives, Glimpses Inside

At times, Tokyo appears like a complex maze of closed-off interiors. Windows, when there are any, are curtained, or turned into walls with huge sliding doors. Walls are many; doors shut tight, and the most one sees of the interior of say, a restaurant, is often the photo on the menu out front. Life in Tokyo, as lively and dynamic as it is, goes on largely hidden from public view.

This basically closed nature always frustrates me. My interest in seeing how Tokyoites live feels restricted and boxed off. My curiosity is aroused when I imagine some inner intrigue going on in some inside space, but I rarely have that curiosity satisfied. Part of the culture shock any westerner feels in Tokyo comes from the eeriness of having so many spaces closed from view.

As a foreigner, the number of interior Tokyo spaces one actually gets a look at is remarkably small. Unlike America, where invitations to other people's homes, schools or offices are common, Tokyoites socialize in public places. I can barely even imagine what even long-term friends' and colleagues' homes look like. Most, I am sure, I will never see. I can remember where we met for coffee, a drink or a meal, but except for public places like that, I have actually seen very little of the hidden inside of Tokyo.

In contrast, I have sharp images of the interiors of Europe and America. People invite you in. Western architecture opens onto streets, squares or visible areas, allowing passersby to gawk and gaze to their heart's content. Even in the verticality of New York, first floors are glassed, front windows large, and looking freely in and out is a major pastime. In large part, that's what you pay for there; in Tokyo, you pay to shutter yourself from outside view.

That is why I love the early dark time of year in Tokyo. For a couple hours on crisp winter evenings, Tokyo exposes itself. From sunset at five to around seven, I can look all I want into interior spaces impossible to see any other time. Daytime glare shields most windows from easy sight, and by seven most shades are pulled, lights dimmed and the city closes itself from view. Only in between day and night is it possible to really see in.

Optimally, a train ride at winter sunset opens a privileged view of what is normally concealed behind doors, dividers, and coverings. The quick-passing slide show of brightly lit interiors lasts only a few seconds each, but from the slight elevation and distance of the train, Tokyo becomes one huge, voyeuristic dollhouse.

Interior spaces lit by fluorescent bulbs become

Slideshow Lives, Glimpses Inside

seconds-long panoramas. Entire lives, families, and homes flash by in successive frames. All the lively dramas of the city act themselves out on boxed little stages spotlighted sharply and clearly, but only for a moment. I relish catching these glimpses of all the places I never go.

Through the windows of company offices, I can see white-shirted workers huddled over interlocked desks amid computers, faxes and copiers. The employees hunker over their postponed work or squirm semi-attentively to the day's final lecture from the boss, pontificating from the front of a room.

The big, plump chairs of hair salons sit empty over piles of different-colored hair cuttings being swept by stylists dressed in tight, chic, black clothing. Long racks in hip boutiques display fashions to meandering shoppers indistinguishable from the clothing hanging on racks except for their body motion. Discount eyeglass and suit shops wait expectant for the last sale, outdoor mannequins and sidewalk tables half-retrieved and pulled inside.

Wives kneel over half-done dinner tables, wip-ing their aprons smooth over their breasts and stomach, glancing at the TV and twisting their eyes to their children. Nursery rooms stand half-empty, with toys, paper, crayons, games and mats tucked onto shelves, teachers wandering a little dazed behind bright-colored posters, oversized letters and animal cut-outs, waiting for the last of the children to be picked up so they can go home.

Then a bit later, salarymen line themselves up along brown bottles of beer already in mid-meal, their cigarette smoke curling up in satisfaction. Fitness-minded, one-hour athletes work their bodies in front of floor-to-ceiling windows at exercise clubs, a bit blurry behind the condensation on the glass, following aerobics commands. Once, I even saw a funeral, with a roomful of mourners in black kneeling in a line towards the altar. It seemed like an unusual thing to leave unveiled, and like all rituals, it was a reminder.

And then suddenly the glaring lights of the station shatter these fleeting images of Tokyo's hidden interior life and return me to myself. In the station, you can only see the station and the inside of the train car, as if a blanket of light is thrown over your vision to keep it from ranging too far.

What Tokyo offers during this free movie-like matinee is perhaps nothing unusual, certainly not shocking. But the flow of exposed interiors and the hasty consideration of each in turn create a wistful feeling for the comfort of being inside and the wintry solitude of being outside. Other large cities are designed around openness and accessibility, but Tokyo is shy about its inside spaces, so each stolen glance becomes a special pleasure.

By seven in the evening, though, most of these day

Slideshow Lives, Glimpses Inside

spaces are closed and the night spaces have their windows covered, the few that have any windows at all. Offices and shops shutter down, homes curtain off privacy, and all the internal scenes are once again secreted away inside. When that happens, my eyes and I feel once again, sadly, half-lidded and excluded.

Both Directions at Once, Change in the City

That Tokyo changes constantly is a truism; but what fascinates me is how and why it changes, and in what directions. To me, Tokyo often seems like a fickle teenager, moodily swapping its clothes every whipstitch. In parts of the city I only sometimes go, multi-storied buildings sprout up and entire stations are carved out seemingly overnight. At times it seems half of Tokyo is shrouded behind the metal walls of construction sites.

The dizzying pace, though, is only part of the change; there's process and purpose there as well. Passing by the same places twice a day on my commute, I see the gradual progression of projects with a kind of time-lapse photography. At Shinjuku station, where my train pauses, construction blazes forward on the busiest station in the world. Once out at my stop, I walk by a temple, where restoration of a sacred spot ambles along at an entirely different pace, and different direction.

Watching these two construction sites, I realize that Tokyo changes both towards the future and back towards the past. The contrast between the station and the temple could hardly be sharper. Yet, Tokyo encompasses both transformations with equal ease.

The upgrade at Shinjuku station is almost purely functional. Aesthetics battles practicalities. A million people a day stride through the cramped maze of intersecting pathways. Even with full-scale construction, it's as busy as ever. To handle that load, logistics takes over: spongy cushions, non-slip rubber mats, safety nets, huge red arrows and signs of apology drape every corner of the station. Beauty takes a back seat to durability. The station prepares for the future.

The temple has it easier. They also remain open, but with the same tranquility as normal. Netting hangs like a cocoon over the ancient wooden buildings. Scaffolding made of thick metal poles and bolted clamps protects the delicate structures inside. The occasional visitor can walk down a temporary metal slope, but the priests remain inside, away from the craftsmen at work restoring ancient dignity. Quietude and reflection suffuse this construction site. Even the clank of hammers and crunch of wheelbarrows calm me as I walk by.

Shinjuku station has just the opposite effect. It always makes me jumpy. Helmeted guards direct the frantic throngs of shoppers, workers, and fun-seekers wandering through the tangled interior of the station towards ma-

Both Directions at Once, Change in the City

terial fulfillment. The station itself continues to expand up and down the tracks—and over and under, sprawling in all directions. More and more of the surrounding area becomes conquered by new exits, walkways, overpasses, underpasses, tunnels, and shortcuts—all, of course, lined by and leading to places of commerce.

The temple, originally built in 1631, has no doubt been scaled down since its founding. Now, a wedding hotel, model apartment showroom and 24-hour *chukka* shop hem in its borders. Inside its bunkered walls, the raw wood, hand painting, and beveled glass of the buildings reflect another vision altogether. The skilled craftsmen, experienced in traditional restoration, work with unhurried steadiness. On my way to work, I like to linger, watching them bend a piece of copper for the roof or smooth a timber for a wall. They move with grace and purpose in their special work pants and big-toed work socks, proud of protecting the past against the future.

In Shinjuku, the workers remain hidden behind metal dividers. As do many of the changes. The finished stage hides all trace of bolts, beams, gutters, raw concrete and water stains. It seems an aesthetic of embarrassment to me, hiding the crude connecters and plain materials. Perhaps for many, the brand-new materials, slick with stain-resistant polymers and bathed in artificial colors, promise a modern life. To me, though, they impart little more than

Beauty and Chaos

an accelerated life and momentary comfort.

In that sense, Shinjuku station is caught up in its own dynamism, the best example of how Tokyoites love change for change's sake. The construction will no doubt finish quickly, but the newness will soon wear off. Tokyoites also love the past, at times with obsessive attention. The improvements at the temple offer permanence and continuity, and reveal the deeply felt need to stay connected to the past.

Though Shinjuku station invites easy cynicism and the temple easy respect, I like both these kinds of change. Even more, I like that both go on simultaneously. Tokyo always seems to me to hold both the future and the past carefully in hand, and always blends an intriguing vision of time into its spatial expression.

Tokyo's Million Marathons

The race contestants are preparing nervously. Their feet paw the ground, eyes staring forward, muscles tense. The train slows, the doors open, the count starts, "On your marks, get set, go! And THEY'RE OFF. It's the daily Tokyo race, to the stairs, to the escalator, to the taxi line, to just about anywhere.

From morning to night, Tokyoites run. Converging on the station in the morning, they break into a run. They rush across crosswalks; shoot through yellow lights; and dash to the office. They run to lunch and back. They stomp up the right-hand side of escalators (the left side being reserved for standing). At night, they flap their arms and legs furiously for the last train, and, once back home, they speed through the station to get in the taxi line. Half of Tokyo seems to be on fast-forward.

Running forms part of the city's rhythm, and its texture. For every train, I see commuters stretching their necks on quick tiptoe in a complex calculus of motion, location, and crowd density. They check when the train will leave from the departure board, determine how many commuters are in their way and how fast they will have to

Beauty and Chaos

go before breaking into a well timed sprint. Everywhere I look in Tokyo I see young women mincing quickly in high heels, men in tie-flying lunges onto the train, duets of women friends hurrying across intersections, and kids in uniforms, their arms in front of them like icebreakers, wiggling through crowds.

All this running is terribly infectious. I confess: I run sometimes, too. Almost unconsciously over the years, I began to conform to this social running habit. Even when I don't run, I feel like it. And I've come to appreciate the nuance of it. When a salaryman, triple-jumping across the platform, shoulders collapsed like a cat, lands inside the train as the doors slam shut behind him, I applaud. I help him pull in his bag, even though every station in the city has signs warning of the dangers of running for trains. I follow the flight of the young woman dashing past me. She's late, it seems, but for what? a date? work? What could be so important to dodge through the crowd like a football fullback? In high heels? How can EVERYone be late?

In Paris, people run, but less so, and anyway, spend hours recovering in cafés. New Yorkers move fast, but are unafraid to be rude, pushy and direct. Strangely, running in Tokyo has a certain politeness to it. It often avoids confrontation. It may not save a lot of time, but it saves a little face. At the most popular meeting spots in the city, like

Tokyo's Million Marathons

Hachiko Square in Shibuya, people will speed up the last few meters towards a waiting friend, propelled by guilt at being late. Twenty meters' running is part of the apology. In the morning and after lunch, workers hasten the last block or two to work. Perhaps in some offices, sweating a little upon arrival is considered a good thing; it shows seriousness of purpose. It shows your schedule is full, and it shows what is important. It shows you ran.

Is all of this a case of nerves? A fear of time? A regression to childhood freedom of motion? Even the grade school nature walks in the park near my house are taken at a pretty good clip. The kids run up along the side of the line, and then fall back into place, before running again, as fast as their little legs will carry them. The kids are clearly excited, but are adults running because they are excited too? Running seems so natural to the kids at such a young age. I suppose they'll need to get in shape for their future. Early training will help.

Even when people are not in full-sprint mode, they take nimble galloping steps like folk dancers, shifting their foot rhythm to fit the distance carefully. Sometimes people will just spontaneously run for a hundred meters or so, and then slow down back to a normally fast walk, seemingly for no reason at all. Maybe it's just a pleasure in itself, a kind of harried city ballet, or a modern dance routine where the audience becomes the dancers on stage. My students tell me, breathless on arrival to class, that they always run because they are always late. I suppose there's a strange kind of logic to that, but how can so much lateness be such a regular part of Tokyo life?

Running is also embedded in Tokyo's fantasy life. Television dramas fill their scripts with running scenes. Good leg muscles seem to be a requirement for a TV acting career. In nearly every show, characters express their resolve—about a relationship, to tell the truth, to undo some mistake—by running. The TV characters jog for kilometers through (surprisingly) empty streets, certain of their dramatic internal resolve. Perhaps in real life, as on TV, running allows the feeling of being, for even just a few minutes of one's own story, goal-directed, decisive and unimpeded by doubt. In Tokyo life, those feelings can be rare.

Every city has its own pockets of irrationality, and running is just part of Tokyo's. It tires you out, even just watching, but creates its own vibrancy. The essence of Tokyo life is forward motion. Running is just the bodily manifestation of that urban impulse. Running enacts the city psyche. Running does save a few minutes, I suppose, and in Tokyo, where time might just be the single most precious commodity, even a few minutes of time is something to cherish and something to run for.

And occasionally when standing calmly on a train

waiting in a station, I will see someone really racing all out down the stairs and rocketing across the platform trying to hop on at the last second. When the door closes just in front of them and all their hurry turns to didn't-make-it disappointment, I find it hard to not snicker like a madman, quietly to myself, and whisper, "Oh, too late!" Watching them trapped back on the platform as my train starts rolling, I always feel selfishly, absurdly, as if their lost time and wasted energy have somehow become my own, without my having had to run at all.

No Time to Spare–Schedules

One evening, I noticed a young woman on the Inokashira line flipping through an amazing series of papers. In succession, she studied her monthly *arubaito* work schedule, train arrival times, bus departure times, her appointment date book, and late night TV schedule. She then pulled out an itinerary for a weekend onsen trip with friends, complete with meeting times, train times, tour times, free time (with a list of shops), and return time.

In the 17 minutes (express) from Shibuya to Kichijoji, she had reviewed where she would be—and when—for the next 30 days. I wondered if her entire life had been so minutely scheduled. I guess it had.

Times and schedules are major preoccupations in Tokyo. Clocks hang everywhere and few wrists go watchless. Wallet-size tripartite schedules for trains and buses are distributed on every metal counter. Stationary stores stock a vast selection of diary and appointment books. Train companies advertise their newly increased speeds in big, bold lettering. I wait for the day when seconds will be added after the minutes on train station platforms detailing arrival and departure times.

Beauty and Chaos

Japanese workers and students are surely the most highly scheduled in the world. Every university has huge bulletin boards devoted to schedules and every Tokyo office has a white board that dominates a wall—or two. Work schedules are fastidiously marked, ordered, and arranged. Just mention a date or time in a meeting and people instinctively reach for their overstuffed appointment books. Students look stricken when coming to class even a couple minutes late; clearly, they've been scolded by angry teachers on "late duty" who stand every morning at school gates all over the country.

I've never quite understood this obsession with time. I suppose it's a little like baths, Japanese relish a kind of cleanliness of time. Open time seems sloppy and confusing. Anyway, people in Tokyo are not used to having much of it. Tokyo is intricately woven together by tight schedules, in part because Tokyoites like to accomplish a lot of things. Schedules help do that. However, the obsession with schedules goes beyond the merely practical. The desire to have every future moment organized becomes a kind of unyielding perfectionism.

To me, such hyper-scheduling feels claustrophobic and inflexibly dull. At times, too, schedule-lovers seem so obsessed with order and control they cannot react with spontaneity or humanity. This attitude holds a certain danger. The fatal train derailment in Hyogo felt all the more tragic

No Time to Spare—Schedules

because of one of the causes—the driver speeding to get back on schedule.

In other countries, being late is not such a big deal. In fact, it's expected, as a normal, if still slightly aggravating, part of being human. In Europe, train workers can go on strike for weeks and EVERYone's late. In most countries around the world, putting up an exacting Japanese-style bus schedule, like some roadside shrine to time, would be considered some kind of bureaucratic joke. Buses come when they come, people are where they are. All too often in Japan, though, people become less important than the dictates of being on time.

Even with millions of numbers written carefully in millions of little slots, Japanese are regularly late. Apologies for being late are as common as good morning or good afternoon. What other country in the world has official apology certificates for late trains? In a country so tightly scheduled, it also seems ironic there is so much overtime. Why doesn't all this tight, careful scheduling allow workers to get out the door on time? Scheduling, it seems, is more ideal than actuality.

I suppose that even if one is late, it's comforting to know what the schedule *should* have been. Schedules look nice and neat compared to Tokyo's unpredictable blur. Tokyo's many time demands are relieved by the comforting control of scheduling, like some massive daily group tour that one can sink into with the soothing reassurance that all will go according to plan—even when it doesn't. Schedules recognize that time is a precious commodity to be frugally saved. To me, though, the city's millions of schedules seem like postal savings accounts—routinely deposited but rarely spent.

Tokyoites can be great time-wasters, though. Anytime anywhere in Tokyo, wandering souls freed from the fetters of a schedule walk aimlessly, stand reading books, window shop, daydream over coffee and generally lose themselves in the feeling of the moment. Outside the rigid economy of time, these human moments become special, secret pleasures. It must be a relief to be off schedule for a change. During these *nonbiri* loafing around times, one not only loses control over the schedule, one renounces it entirely.

Ultimately perhaps, the illusion of control over time that schedules offer is a fragile one, about as reliable as having your palm read. Though Tokyoites, like train timekeepers, try harder and perhaps succeed more often in scheduling their city than any other in the world, ultimately, urban life just doesn't fit into any tedious schedule. For me, one of Tokyo's most fascinating aspects is this ongoing tussle between the idealism of meticulously ordered time and the delightful tug of unpredictable human disorder.

Part Four

Beauty and Chaos, Slices and Morsels of Tokyo Life

Souvenirs from the Land of Impulse–Don Quixote

Just finding the entrance to Don Quixote is disorienting, well-guarded as it is by stacked trays of Pez dispensers, boxes of chocolate covered macadamia nuts, and columns of oversized coffee cans. Free-for-all piles of snorkeling gear and rows of aluminum camping chairs hide a clear view inside. Between all these, shoppers can just slip in and squeeze out of Don Quixote's consumer labyrinth.

Certainly the most intense, jumbled and overwhelming store in a city that's the same, Don Quixote encapsulates a certain aspect of Tokyo's character: the overcrowded, plastered-over, ever-practical, consumption-obsessed, architecturally chaotic, throwaway intensity of hovering right up to the brink of total sensory overload.

A new variation in retailing, Don Quixote is the wild cousin of the 100-yen shops, 1000-yen clothing shops, Uniqlo, vending machine plazas, and convenience stores that have sprouted in every half-unused space in the city. Don Quixote's shrine fair atmosphere, though, makes the average corner convenience store feel like a Zen meditation hall.

Once inside, every conceivable space holds goods and more goods. Half-hidden metal grates stretch up the walls sprouting smiley face scented deodorizers, bosom and butt shaped lighters, red flicker light bulbs, pink kitty nail clippers, Indian incense, glow-in-the-dark characters, 3-D stickers, key rings that both pop open beer cans and peel oranges (a common combination one wonders).

Shelves overflow with cardboard boxes stuffed with pajamas, backpacks, cotton underwear, plastic wiffle-ball bats, and lacey underwear. In that order. A floor-standing cage brims over with pink, orange, green, blue stuffed giraffes, elephants, dogs, fish and unidentifiable animals—perhaps the result of genetically manipulated stuffing.

Even the floor offers little stability. Plastered over the entirety are big, white arrows pointing towards bargains and orange-yellow-pink hand-scrawled signs covered in shiny strips of clear tape. Dance-step foot-shapes point in different directions through the maze. Elevator doors, too, are covered, decipherable as doors only when the Day-Glo *katakana* signs accordion open briefly, imploringly. Of course, the walls of the elevator are coated in more cheery encouragement to spend.

Overhead hovers an artificial jungle. Hanging like thick vegetation are rows of silk Chinese dresses and gently swaying circles of plastic-wrapped ties (300 yen and

Souvenirs from the Land of Impulse—Don Quixote

just as ugly). Three-meter-long, bean-filled snakes languidly wait to thump the inattentive forehead. Sinuous gray hoses of colored lights hang like vines (300 yen per meter). Long lines of hand-in-hand plastic monkeys reach down mischievously (500 yen for two). A string of Tabasco bottle lights loop down next to a string of hooked fish lights (3,000 yen a string). Beach balls blown up in convenient string carriers (cheaper than at the beach) bounce around the shoulders. Dangling soccer balls roped with nylon mesh need a solid header out of the way to get by.

Avoiding contact with things is impossible, of course. Bumping into things is part of the ploy. Everything's at hand. Movement is slow. The flung-around discontinuities feel like a busy week's worth of clothes tossed on a chair. The shelves are too close, never allowing any objective point of view. No vantage point offers relief or the hope of an overview. Everything is right in your face. The impression of variable visual concatenation at every angle disrupts, delights and eventually exhausts. Visually, it's not one big store, it's a million.

Tripping over a stack of DVD players while reaching for cold medicine but ending up with a hand on affordable garden tools blurs any distinction between needs and wants. Ordered searching for an item slips in significance to the sheer cathartic bursting of categorical order. Nothing is where it should be. It is just where it is. You don't

Beauty and Chaos

find what you want; you want what you find.

The third floor holds electronics and miniatures in phenomenally incoherent juxtapositions. Cascading clip racks of bunched up underwear, cartoon ties, and metal socket sets surround a display shelf of talking cemetery ghost heads, which chatter unintelligibly for a few seconds above large, open-mouthed washing machines. Sleek Maglite flashlights dribble down a wall rack in order of size and power. Batteries, of course, are found on another floor.

Radios and alarm clocks in sleek box shapes, multicolored, and complexly dialed, wait unplugged. Next to this practicality, lava lamps bubble in oily profusion beside a large selection of hand-held vacuum cleaners. Extension cords hang coiled over by the register. An extensive collection of pricey lighters fills a museum-like glass case, well lit and well locked. Across from the case is an even larger case filled with sharkskin men's handbags, gold belt buckles and white collared dress shirts.

The mind searches for order, and is keenly resisted. The mind has trouble even finding words to identify most of the goods. In Don Quixote, though, words are unneeded. It's the land of things, racing at you in unexpected order.

In the next diorama, bras different from the first floor bras hang unfulfilled next to a stack of ski poles next to a box of leather dress gloves next to a stack of metal camp-

Souvenirs from the Land of Impulse—Don Quixote

ing stoves. Perfumes inside a glass cabinet are tucked behind the stoves above which hovers an 11,200-yen clinging, Budweiser girl miniskirt, in a range of sizes. Is this the outdoor section? The clothing section? But, in Don Quixote, there is nothing so organized as to be called a "section."

The stairwells back downstairs are transformed into a pop-culture poster gallery: sneering Clash; unshaved Kurt Cobains; the Doors next to peyote-button cactus; Bob Marley with a cigar-sized spliff; the Sex Pistols spitting; Jimi Hendrix posters, though, are over by the blacklights. Don Quixote is a postmodern museum of pop culture. Here, surface is everything; depth, nothing.

Downstairs, the basement floor displays an unbelievably immense variety of snack packages and perhaps the single largest collection of instant noodles and canned drinks in the entire world. I suppose that is something to be proud of, but I'm not sure. Nothing else sold there takes much more preparation than instant noodles nor lasts as long as a canned drink.

Even while wrapping itself in the banners of practicality, convenience, and low pricing, ultimately most of what you buy (and you do buy) at Don Quixote are simply souvenirs from the land of impulse. Of course, most items in Don Quixote make life, home and play more comfy, livable, lively, amusing, and somehow, in a roundabout way

Beauty and Chaos

(the only way there is at Don Quixote), more human.

Tokyoites love shopping, or rather, they love shopping experiences. Don Quixote offers a super-concentrated one that departs from Tokyo's usual approach. Most Tokyo stores offer one style, one type of goods or a certain distinct atmosphere. They feel a relief from the mixed-up, oddly combined areas of the city. What Don Quixote sells, though, is that hard-to-commodify experience—the chaos of the city itself.

Elegant Eating–the Art of Chopsticks

Unlike some people from knife-and-fork countries, I never had difficulty using chopsticks. But, the manipulation of two little sticks is not so interesting in itself; what really intrigues me is the entire chopstick culture. Using chopsticks combines the satisfaction of repetition with the stunning beauty of visual representation. They emphasize the performative and aesthetic side of eating, rather than the crude biological necessity of nutrition.

It's not only a different way of eating; it's a different way of experiencing food. When the food is transferred to the mouth by chopsticks, there is a brief instant when the food hangs in the air, gently held in place by its temporary frame. At this instant, visual pleasure briefly supplants, and then augments, the pleasure of tasting. Eating with a knife and fork is just eating with the mouth, but eating with chopsticks is eating with the eyes first, and then the mouth.

The frame created by the chopsticks, open on the mouth end, closed on the finger-fist side, suggests a film frame. The dish-framed food is repeatedly broken apart into smaller, wood-framed pieces, which pass one by one in front of the eyes before disappearing inside. Only so much food fits between a pair of thin, pointy, little sticks. Working the chopsticks is a delicate, nimble process, requiring coordination and concentration, but not looking as you do so is missing the whole point.

The chopsticks enact the food, display it, and energize it. Everything wiggles in the air. This re-created motion is clearest especially when eating uncooked foods, which are so common in Japan, and complement chopsticks well. Pieces of fish, especially fish, become re-animated by the motion towards the mouth. The *sashimi* lives swimmingly again for a moment before being tucked away.

But even crackly, deep-fried *tempura* shrimp are temporarily re-born. Small white slivers of pulled apart fish—steaming—seem to wiggle all the more before being popped inside. Dense packets of sticky rice sway for one last moment before performing rice's purifying and satiating role. Long disobedient strings of *natto* require a circular flourish of the arm to recapture escaping threads. Vegetables quiver in warmth and color.

This movement also presents different angles of the food to the eater's eyes. It allows one to see the near side as well as the far side of the morsel, an entire three-dimensional area. The texture, wetness, floppiness, color,

Elegant Eating—the Art of Chopsticks

and steam all present themselves up close with chopsticks in a way that would be considered rude if done with a fork.

Using a knife and fork, in contrast, quickens consumption. Food is cooked, cut, poked, delivered. They work without the elaborate ritual dance. They make eating into serious, un-playful surgery. Of course, chopsticks can also mechanically shovel in wads of *ramen*, half-bowls of rice, or chunks of beef, but look around any "Japanese" restaurant in Tokyo and what hits your eyes is a prancing, delighted ballet of sticks in the air.

Chopsticks dramatize eating. They wave around, hug pieces of food good-bye, jump around to make points and then clack down to rest. They choreograph magnificent performances. In looking across the space of the restaurant, the communal lofting of pieces of food up into space transforms the restaurant into a kind of auditorium, with tables transformed to stages, each with its own choreographed dance of food. Tokyoites are almost never as lively and demonstrative as with chopsticks in hand.

This chopstick ballet is, like real ballet, a kind of writing and re-writing of objects in space. Scholars have even suggested that chopsticks arrived in Japan at the same time as brushes for ink writing. The food is written into the air, then into the body, placed there as if by the hand of another, distant enough to maybe be an imagined parent feeding one again. Chopsticks turn the pleasure of eating

Beauty and Chaos

back to that forgotten time of being fed, of being the object while feeling like the subject. Children, after all, spend as much time playing with and looking at food as they do actually eating it.

Chopsticks are not your own fleshy hand of course, but are certainly not a cold, metallic tool. They are more pencil than scalpel—a cultural magic wand. The body's own chopsticks, the forearm is composed of two parallel bones that move in similar fashion. Chopsticks mimic the functioning of the radius and ulna inside the human arm. Whenever I use chopsticks, I feel this elemental, primal pull, and enjoy the food more fully. Everyone else seems to as well.

Chopsticks, too, have a holistic side, their own sort of harmony. After and between use, chopsticks are never laid down apart. Rather, they are always placed, and re-placed together, lined up exactly. Chopsticks laid down, uncrossed, side by side, on the top of the bowl, on a fold of paper, on the chopsticks rest or on the side of a plate, are always, always together, as if one entity, finally, again.

What Goes Around Comes Around— Pachinko

The lack of movement, the fixing of the self, butt on seat, hand on knob, elbow in air, while the silver balls flurry around with crashing, tortured constancy is a unique experience. Fixing a coin into the crevice of the grip reduces the last hint of tactile control. You watch. The balls fly, drop, and bounce—gravity endlessly repeated. It's bland, unskilled, repetitive to the point of idiocy, but all of that is perhaps the point, the frisson, the kick behind the kick. In Tokyo with its myriad expensive pleasures, pachinko is the simplest and most concrete.

Of course that's what makes it so complex and otherworldly.

The silver balls shooting up and splashing down over the array of pins is the central sensual pleasure of pachinko. The flashing, flickering lights, the rippling, splashing bulbs, the bells, ringers and cartoon noises all blur into an overload of input that glues you to your seat.

The whole operation is a mini-carnival, loud, flashy and enlivening. The senses are taken captive. The presence of other people, packed in shoulder to shoulder, passionately smoking, drowned into wordlessness is just noticeable above the ceaseless rush of mechanical whirling, hitting, pumping, tapping. No hint of the human voice ever rises above the din, only ecstatic bursts of rhythmic patter, then a crashing reverse in direction, a rapid modulation of pitch, a jump in tone, the brutal severing of melodic connection, the intentional disruption of coherence.

It is the experiential sound of an infinite number of inexperienced musicians playing an infinite number of primitive instruments. The pink, plink, plunk of the balls on the pins combine into waves of in-phase and out-of-phase noise. It is noise in the purest sense: noise for noise's sake. You contribute to the irritating cacophony without being responsible. The noise you create at your own individual machine combines with the noise of everyone else in the place. The height of the machines keeps everyone from seeing over them to the next aisle, while the walls echo the noise perfectly and relentlessly into an unfocused but potent wall of glaringly white noise.

The colors of the lights are bright, distinct and varied. Reds, oranges and yellows predominate, but blues and greens also leap out from the machines. The colors offer a garishly shocking contrast with the subtle colors common in most Japanese homes, restaurants and neigh-

What Goes Around Comes Around—Pachinko

borhoods. The colors are drawn from the same symbolic color schemes as the colors of shrine festivals, young girls' kimonos, animation, fast food restaurants, and other sites given to the quick allocation of eyeful pleasure.

The visual and aural collide in circles of cascading on-and-offs, pinwheels of yellows, bright-pink flashes, and exploding reds. The distorting reflections of curved, polished pillars at the ends of aisles, sheets on overhead sidewalls, and bars along counters shout their gleaming silver alloy. They act like funhouse mirrors, contorting all motion caught in their reflective surfaces.

Thick smoke hangs like clouds of barely contained impatience, muting all of the colors. The cheap, burned tobacco inflames the nostrils and invades your being with every breath. Tears form, but unlike the balls, never drop, re-emphasizing pachinko's essential, choking melancholy.

The most erotic aspect of pachinko is the opening wide of small, stubby, loin-like levers. They coyly spread, and then tighten back up, so that only a perfect hit can enter and produce, or reproduce, more balls from the spout below. The missed hits fall wasted into the sad, little, draining hole at the farthest bottom of the machine.

The density of the balls is equaled in perfection by their slippery, constant flow. They are just the right size to move just right. The plastic handle that launches the balls, though, is over-large, reinforcing the infantilizing qualities of the entire experience. You can grip it only with a full pterodactyl spread of your hand.

Pachinko obsesses over the illusion that repetition will lead to mastery. There seems to be a kind of control over the ball, but not really. The balls go where they want to, in a mechanical parody of self-will. It is the repetition compulsion taken to its obvious conclusion. The little bit of imprecision, the slightly different bounce of the ball hitting the same pins, captivates. Why did that one bounce over there? Then there? The different weight of the ball? The different propulsive force of the mechanism? Pachinko demands an unusual mixture of patience, optimism and compulsiveness.

The tedious attention to the set patterns of pins, the subtle positioning of the handle, calculating the exact pop and bounce to hit the big pay-back hole right in the middle, and the print-out of numbers on the counter above the machine form a self-contained sphere of meaning. Pachinko is a meaning-defying, wordless production, silent in its noise, an inversion of the highly predictable sounds, colors, patterns, experiences of everyday life. It is a reversal of the surface of life, a kind of exposure of the interior Brownian motion, a topography of random motion.

Though pachinko seems meaningless, incessant and loud, the crudest of leisure activities, it has its soothing, meditative aspect as well. The rounded vault of the ma-

What Goes Around Comes Around—Pachinko

chines surround faces, figures, and geometric shapes composed in themes of movies, jungle animals, horse racing, and detective mysteries. These images whirl by on tiny, just-out-of-focus screens, stopping to taunt with potential point values, then moving on quickly.

These flowing images form an extensive iconography devoted to the representation and worship of chance. In these days of computerized video games, pachinko stands as an ancient ritual of gaming. It is analog fun in an age of digital dominance, strangely without a fantasy side beyond the hope of hitting the jackpot.

It's that that's most honest about pachinko—that money, work, time, the whole vertical layout of life is simply a gamble after all, a bounce of the silver ball, again and again and again.

The Tradition of Banners

On every long vertical building in Tokyo, pulled tight from holders top and bottom along the dull, flat ends of visible buildings float streams of long colored cloth packed with characters, pictures, images, and icons in bursts of communicative meanings and markings. On every commercial street, pushing out onto the sidewalks and walk ways stand shorter, perkier banners fluttering on poles stuck in base-stands.

These banners animated by the natural force of the air, bring together Tokyo's vertical inclination with its commercial orientation. In this day and age of neon, LCD, projectors and every conceivable computerized display, these banners feel like a curious throwback to an ancient time. But like many traditional remnants of old Edo, they have an impact and a fascination that modernized crafts cannot quite achieve.

Banners announce the uses of space and act as standing invitations. In addition to announcing the opening or renewal of shops, restaurants, bars, clubs, and pachinko parlors, which change often enough, banners also announce seasonal exhibits of art, clothes sales, seasonal food, festivals, fairs, bargains and any other event for which temporality is a sign of quality. Banners are traditional also in their confident merchant-like solicitation, a polite display of the good faith of the seller. Their form fits their purpose.

The longer banners—some stretch two or three stories—catch the eyes of passersby who glance up at the buildings from a distance, across a square, bus and taxi rotary, station platform, or from any angle. Tokyo generally has few of these full frontal positions due to the compact density of buildings, but banners always work from a distance. They work as huge announcements to a wide-open space and call up some of the grandeur of distance, which is a relative luxury in Tokyo. Banners feel like imperial decrees.

After getting used to the displays, one ritually reads them, anxious to know what could be important enough to announce across four or five stories of space. The most impressive banners are typically on the larger department stores, which announce a variety of festivities, in keeping with their role of expanding service in their stores beyond simple sales. In that sense, the banners seem to announce a community activity that one can participate in. Large entertainment complexes, whether city run or privately owned, also feature banners of varying sizes over their architectural bodies, telling of museum exhibits or special shows.

The Tradition of Banners

As much kite-like as sign-like, the crucial element of banners is their motion, a subtle flickering, floating, and dancing. At any time of year the colors are chosen appropriately, the announcements coherent to seasonal concerns, holidays, exhibits, feelings, but it is the calming, wave-like motion that appeals most deeply to me. They make buildings come alive.

Smaller banners mark out a territory in front of smaller shops, catching the eye that might glance down a street in search of a *ramen* shop, or the notice of a bicyclist who will return to a half-hidden little liquor store or rice shop later on. New stores often boast huge areas of these banners, saving on the electric bills for a neon sign by letting the wind do all the work of motion, and encouraging passersby with a visual *"irrashaimase!"*

As a westerner used to reading only left to right, I especially like how the writing runs from top to bottom. This moves my eye in the direction down towards the entrance. The banners act like directional signals where anyone can fit in comfortably under the massive spell cast by these consumer proclamations. To enter a building is to be pulled, along with one's energy, cash, interests and attention span into an interior space toward a goal, usually a goal of fun. Banners never announce onerous or troublesome activities, after all.

Banners are cousins to *noren*, the hanging pieces of

cloth that mark space and offer shade just outside the doors of more traditional shops and restaurants. Like noren, they act on several levels simultaneously. First, they comfort, by being traditional material; second, they inform and create meaning; and third, they decorate what might otherwise be a bland and unappealing front, like a bright scarf thrown over a clothes outfit for accent.

Traditionally, in Japan, long streams of cloth mark things of importance. The kimono is most importantly wrapped by a huge winding of cloth around the stomach-womb of the woman's figure. Cloth is traditionally made in long pieces whose colors are set by dipping in rivers. Like kimonos, banners are coverings that invite and entice by symbolically covering up what's inside, thereby appealing to the desire for what cannot be seen.

In other places, too, cloth has other similar effects. Apartment buildings are draped on sunny days by sheets, futons, blankets hung out to dry. Of course, this hanging to dry is a practical household necessity, but it creates a spectacular effect when, on a sunny day, entire mansions seem covered in cloth, as if in celebration together. So, too, does cloth mark everything from sumo to funerals, and in the distant past, the position of an army.

I always wonder if these banners are recycled somehow or simply thrown out to be burned. The massive investment of time and effort seems excessive for poten-

The Tradition of Banners

tially little pay-off, compared to other, surer methods of advertising. So, other principles, of desire, of pleasure, and of work are as important as simply bringing in paying customers. Banners are the face of places, and perhaps, like worn-out national flags, are burned in reverent ritual, rather than tossed in the trash.

The Summer Whispers and Calls

At the beginning of summer, I find myself, like most Tokyoites, fumbling for umbrellas, wiping off sweat and shivering under freezing-cold air conditioning. Less noticeable among these seasonal shifts, but just as characteristic, is the change in the city's sounds. Windows open and air seems to conduct sound waves more efficiently. What other seasons mute, summer amplifies.

A city's noises are as inseparable from its character as its buildings or people, so summer is an excellent chance to really hear the city. What I find most fascinating about Tokyo's aural character is the magical transformation from the loud, mechanical assault of the beginning of the season to a natural and calming humanness by the end.

Tokyo's small spaces keep sounds near. Sputtering carburetors, whirling air conditioning fans and omnipresent construction are all so close it makes me jump. High heels, a summertime addiction, are thin as chopsticks but loud as kendo swords. Though fashion is rarely fatal, I have mistaken their piercing ricochet through stairwells for a gunshot more than once.

Tokyo's many eerily disembodied voices also speak at

Beauty and Chaos

way too high a volume. Inside buses, the recorded barrage of stop names, thanks, cautions, and warnings resound in sharp mechanical cadences. I am always embarrassed when I top up my Suica train card; the machine shouts out commands so loud I reach to cover the speaker. Train announcements communicate in melody, with each train line boasting its uniquely urgent tune in shrill upper-register tones. I hear these melodies float all the way from the closest station on summer evenings, ugly and practical.

The most distinctive of sounds, though, is surely the morning whacking of futon set out to dry. The whap-whap of this uniquely Japanese habit fills the air on sunny summer mornings. I think housewives smack the futons much harder than necessary to get rid of the dust—relieving their frustrations and sending out a mysterious drum-like message.

Despite these irritations, somewhere in the middle of summer, everything shifts. Sounds soften and relax. Maybe it's the heat finally taking its toll, as if even noises get *natsubate* summer exhaustion.

Around bonus time, recycle trucks drive through neighborhoods asking for old appliances. The loudspeaker cuts right through thin Japanese walls, but provides a helpful function, coming around twice before carrying off old mechanical friends. The "children return home" announcement that pours out of park, school and playground

The Summer Whispers and Calls

speakers reminds me of my own childhood reluctance to quit playing and go home to dinner. The recorded tones are quite different, though, from my mother's voice or the loud bell my aunt rang to call me home.

By August, the city slips even further into distinctive summer sounds. Crickets start their nighttime opera, turning each evening into a haiku. Surprisingly loud, the many different varieties of Japanese cricket voices become a sleepy soundtrack. The household fan drones lazily in response; and I love to hear that special "shush-shush" as I move around on the mats.

Few people in Tokyo live out of earshot of at least one fireworks display. Since fireworks are restricted to one single day in the U.S., it seems like the Fourth of July comes every week in August. The popping and exploding, even when the visual spray of sparks is out of sight, entertain with faraway, erratic rhythms.

Of course, summer nights invite *bosozoku* motorcycle gangs like moths to a porch light. Their loud, angry exhaust pipes shatter summer nights where sleep comes late and lightly. Though police have curbed them in many areas, I suppose we all have our own fantasied punishment for them. I'd like to see them set to community service, training to be quiet all those yipping dogs that summer's heat provokes to ceaseless self-expression. Or they could be sealed in a soundproof garage with the equally aggressive pre-election campaign trucks.

And then at *Obon* holidays, suddenly everything is turned down another notch, as if someone suddenly hit the mute button on the city's remote control. During this week of startlingly quiet contrast, Tokyo empties out, drivers slow down, and trains run empty without bothering to announce much of anything. Even the crows, the *bosozoku* of birds, seem to be on holiday.

And inside that quietude, one hears again the soft shoe steps and hemming-hawing of human beings, whose more personal and individual noises had been hidden in the huge orchestral volume of the early summer city. That near-silence, the sonic pause of *Obon*, becomes a singular expression of Tokyo's aural character, a soothing late-summer restorative after the raucous noise of early urban summer.

Bathing in Kanji-Hanging Menus

When I first came to Japan, I ate in an *izakaya* entirely wallpapered in magnificent calligraphy. The names of dishes stretched around the room like an ancient temple mural. As I started scribbling down the words to look up later, a Japanese couple beside me noticed what I was doing and started chatting. Since they didn't know some of the dishes either, they became slightly flustered, and had to ask the waiter to cover their embarrassment. After a couple more drinks, even they wrote down a couple names to look up later at home. Dinner had become vocabulary study.

From then on, I love having menus floating above my head as I eat. Only in Japan, I realized, do diners relish reading the names of dishes, written all around them in graceful characters, as much as they enjoy chomping into their food.

Ironically, these menus are the inverse reflection of the plastic food displays that grace many restaurant front windows. This Japanese plastic food is well known among foreign travelers, but the menus on walls inside are even more amazing. From plastic food to word, and from word to plastic food, object and language are tightly connected in an intriguing interplay of ideograms, with real food squeezed in between.

Hanging menus are strikingly common, much like Tokyo's ubiquitous outdoor signs. Not only do they decorate *izakaya* and *nomiya* drinking places, but noodle shops, sushi bars, Chinese-style places and even some western-ish places. These hanging signs enhance the appetite by highlighting the food, acting as a kind of linguistic condiment. Without reading the signs in Japan, half the beauty of eating is lost.

Restaurants in the west have nothing like that. Chalkboards at carryout restaurants are common enough, but to sit beneath elegant, fluid handwriting is rare. Western menus are individual private affairs. The menu is placed into your hands, folds out like a wall divider, and then, after ordering once, and once only, the menus are discreetly handed back into the care of the wait staff. Sharing, much less publicly sharing, a gigantic wall-size menu, is just not part of the process. It's divide and order, every eater for themselves. In Japan, every diner is on the same page and the page is on the wall.

Of course, hanging menu signs, usually without the price, could be considered just a practical ploy to encourage more ordering. That's certainly true, and most dining is done in successive rounds, but there's more to it than

Bathing in *Kanji*—Hanging Menus

that. Japanese often combine their passions, in fact they always do, and here, reading and eating merge into a poetry of the culinary. One of my favorite sake places has the entire wall, to rough wood ceiling, covered in *washi* handmade paper all inscribed with handwriting. These carefully arranged strips of beautiful, delicate paper contain Buddhist moral advice, drinking innuendos, regional statements of pride, and poetic phrases—all the names of various sake brands. You have to be fairly literate, even erudite, just to order. Eating, drinking and reading these names is like immersing oneself in an ancient poem, a visual *furo* bath of *kanji* characters.

Typically, though, the wall menu signs are done in a vigorous *mingei* folk art style, with subtle attention to detail: grass style for elegant complex dishes, chunky *kanji* for hearty *yakitori* chicken skewers, or prim, small characters for appetizers. Many traditional places have wooden plaques hanging from hooks, often burnished by smoke and lacquered in congealed oil from the open grill. A few places use pre-printed paper from beer companies, common at cheaper, heartier places, but most go with simple black ink on pure white paper. The characters are carefully drawn, I imagine, during the afternoon break by the best calligrapher working in the place. At my favorite sake place, the owner blushes with pride at his own calligraphic style. The casual appearance is actually quite studied and displayed with unobtrusive pride.

The effect on diners is tremendous. Everyone constantly eyeballs the names of dishes. Wherever one sits, wherever one looks, a potential order awaits. This ease of ordering is comforting, like having your mother there to cook, but also slightly disturbing, as there is always more to be had. To be biting, for example, into a *tebasaki* chicken wing just as you read a small sign recommending the special handmade dumpling *gyoza tebasaki*, is to suffer a tantalizing disappointment. I constantly think, "Oh, I should have ordered that!" I never leave without having already planned out my choices for the next time I will go.

Interestingly, with all the *kanji* hanging overhead, even the arrangement and configuration of dishes start to look like *kanji*. It's as if the writing determines the actual shapes of the food. *Yakitori* chicken skewers are served up in meaningful *kanji*-like strokes of chicken, grilled fish forms a sinuous ideogram punctuated by a dot of *daikon* radish, and tofu floats in a well-placed pattern of garnishes. It's as if the food evolved out of the language—or maybe the other way around. You read the *kanji* on the wall, and then you "read" the food on the dish.

The feeling, though, is more than the fun of ordering one by one over and over. Wall menus enhance and accentuate the entire experience of the restaurant. The writing expands the interior space like mirrors lining the walls,

Bathing in *Kanji*—Hanging Menus

creating the illusion of a much larger experiential space. The paper keeps things simple, with the passing casualness of a street stall, while the writing transforms the walls into the slippery abstractions of the immense world of words. It's like eating in the middle of a culinary language dictionary, one well worn with regular use.

At the same time, these hanging menus also refocus attention on the taste and smell and texture of the food itself. You may never quite become totally lost in the eating experience, as the word for what you're eating draws you back from your senses, but you taste everything all the more strongly for that. Reading and eating together engages the eternal paradox between the sensory experience of the world and its encapsulation in the abstractions of language. Both these directions have their own appeal, and Japanese places serve them both together.

Pink Power

The other day on the train, a woman across from me was blanketed in pink: pink jacket, pink skirt, hot pink lipstick, white top that reflected the surrounding pink, and pink purse out of which poked a pink wallet. Though I couldn't see, I felt sure she had a pink cellphone, like so many other women in Tokyo. The strange thing was, after living in Tokyo, I found this outfit perfectly normal. I realized that in Japan, pink is an entire aesthetic category in and of itself.

Every country has a visual sense of color that is unique, but in Japan, the one color that stands out is pink. Few other countries use the color pink so often, or in so many ways. All-pink clothing, signs, storefronts, toys and even pink toilet slippers dot the city like chicken pox.

Pink gets its special position because it partakes of cuteness—a concept indispensable to understanding Japanese culture. Few other colors are so inherently cute. Many objects may be cute though the color does not make them so, but paint something pink, and presto, it's cute. In Japan, pink is always cute in and of itself. It brings out the *kawaii* cutesy response, a reaction that is almost always positive.

In the west, cute often holds many kinds of connotations. Pink is positive there too, but with qualifications, as if too childish, too easy, or not expressing oneself quite honestly. It's too babyish. In America, even the custom of buying pink clothes for baby girls has started to change. Pushing a color on a baby only because of the baby's gender is now considered the beginning of a lifetime of sexist treatment. Pink is thought too confining and has come to be avoided.

In Japan, though, girls from birth are surrounded with pink, like special insulation. Pre-school girls ride in pink-cushioned child seats behind their mothers. Step into a girl's clothing section at a store and it glows pink. I guess many schools continue with school uniforms simply to keep the classrooms from becoming awash in pink. For many young girls, weekdays mean dull blue uniforms, while weekends open up for pink sneakers, pink manga characters, pink bikes and shopping for, well, for pink.

Pink connotes innocent femininity and childhood cuteness even for older women. The all-pink woman I saw on the train was around 40 years old. The ladies' kiosk in the middle of Shinjuku station is called 'pi-osku' for 'pink kiosk.' A pink winter scarf turns a black-jacketed woman into an early-spring cherry blossom. Pink is put to hard work to stand out to catch the eye, to bring up

Pink Power

something from the past.

From a western perspective, pink seems almost the visual equivalent of fast food, easy and over-advertised. It feels like a color that one should grow out of. To mark oneself as too feminine seems coy or passive. Western women may occasionally use pink as an accent or to create a certain ironic effect, but in Japan, pink actively demarcates liveliness of a feminine, and only feminine, nature.

Pink is used in a surprising number of advertisements and signs. In parts of Harajuku or Shibuya, every other boutique is doused entirely in pink. These aggressively pink storefronts seem to shout out, "Hey girls, cute, cute things on sale inside!" You know it has cute things even before you look. Teenage girl fashion floats in on a sea of pinkness.

Yet, pink ironically is used in other places, of course, to attract men. Pink's "other" nature comes out in its use in the sex trade. Adult toy stores, ticket porn shop sellers and sex-related businesses all slather themselves in pink. It's the same pink, but inverted, with none of the same feeling innocence or youth, but rather is steeped in just the opposite.

Pink is an unusual color, especially considering how sedate Japanese colors are everywhere else. Cars tend to be white, grey or black. Business suits are typically bland and inconspicuous. Homes and buildings are painted from a limited palette of unobtrusive colors, so dull as to lack specific color words. They're just, well, grayish. It is as if all the flashiness of Japan becomes invested in one color—pink—which does more than its share of visual work to brighten Tokyo's restrained color scheme.

The bright flashiness of pink also feels a little imported. Though foreign clothing stores have recently popularized more English color words, pink is maybe the oldest and most common *gairaigo* color word of them all. Pink takes the bold, open expressive feeling of what is imagined of the west and combines it with a traditional idea of soft femininity. It's a western color, imported for local use.

Somehow, though, pink tries too hard. Traditional words like *momoiro* peach color or *sakurairo* cherry blossom color have a very different connotation, and a different connection to that essential symbol, the cherry blossom. Pink, though, is a color lost in between. It's not quite western, but far from being traditional. It has a little red, a little white, but not too much of either. And because of that, though pink always packs in a certain degree of springtime flavor to it, it always holds a certain sadness in it, too.

Floating in a Sea of Words

Tokyo is a city awash in words. Wherever the eye falls, words reply—advertising, directions, markers, pleas and wild whoops of communicative joy. For a culture that is supposed to value silence, Japanese city walls are surprisingly noisy. Though Hong Kong and other Asian cities also layer on thick visual plasters, Tokyo has so many forms of writing so carefully presented in so many different places that it forms an essential infrastructure of the city's communicative flow and characteristic meaning.

To find the same number of words as the average Tokyoite stumbles past daily on billboards, screens, windows, poles and random unexpected spots, a Londoner would have to enter a library, a New Yorker a newsstand. Despite hard work in those other world cities by glitzy advertisers and graffiti artists, public spaces there remain relatively quiet. Tokyo's walls, in contrast, are frantic with conversation, lively with passing debate, and creatively enveloped in meanings, ideas and possibilities. The average day in Tokyo's word-drenched space demands the equivalent read of a novel's worth of words.

Though Tokyoites often close their eyes or look away

Beauty and Chaos

to shut out the constant assault of words, just as often, they fight words with words, picking up a book or magazine, or pecking at cell phone email to direct the stream of words for themselves. More often, though, they allow themselves to tumble into the incessant ebb and flow of writing all around them and read.

In Tokyo, writing splashes onto space in starry constellations. Blobs and chunks of writing sprout like moss. Stations wear *kanji* two or three meters tall. Train doors tuck in teensy token warnings. Gaudy eateries in Kabukicho splatter windows and invade sidewalks with overstuffed signs; the fronts of Ginza's chunky post-war buildings are edged with well-dressed signs stretching up in neat, little rows like zippers. In parts of Ikebukuro, the buildings are hardly visible at all, with signs and menus squared off in a monstrous visual shouting match.

In even the calmest residential areas, telephone poles have long ago been wrapped in metal plaques with arrows pointing to clinics, soba shops and mom-and-pop appliance stores. The sidewalks and fences near outlying stations are wired with small, framed signs made of plastic or paper stretched over the poles. These temporary *yatai* street stalls of writing boast of newly opened pachinko parlors or local hostess bars in bouncy, childish shapes colored with artificiality. Strangely, the exact same kind of frame is used to display serious black calligraphy directing readers toward funerals. These two vastly differing styles of writing direct and yet disrupt. They show the way, but also reveal, for all to read, the inmost feelings and confusing human needs, from desire to solemn fearful respect.

The relative absence of writing in the new mega-complexes sprouting up in Tokyo is one of their most curious, and alien, features. These new buildings squeeze their writing into straitjackets of condensed rectangles on small, lighted boards set securely in bland lobbies. This writing feels too strictly controlled, as if brutally tamed. The small corralled signs there feel like deflated balloons, drained of all potential. Without the slap in the face, the seductive whispering, the dramatic multiple meanings, it holds very little feeling. One reads them too, but hardly responds.

The rest of the city takes pride in its writing. Writing lowers itself less often to commercial come-on than it aspires to urban art: the chalked-out specials of a small Italian restaurant; the elegant cursive on a hair salon window; the frank chunkiness of a *manga kissaten*'s name. Even *gyudon* shops and convenience stores have their own aesthetic that aims for quick, cheap and easy interaction. The writing demands, threatens, shows off, and distracts, but eventually reveals the whole gamut of emotional variety wrapped around its central core—a love of writing in all its forms. Writing somehow compensates for the cold, disinterested attitude Tokyoites feign by externalizing passion.

Beauty and Chaos

All this written expressiveness could not be motivated by just practical impulse. Japan is a highly literate culture that relishes, and respects, writing. The welter of words reflects a heightened embrace of the most abstract elements of life—time and space. Writing is a loving way of sculpting emptiness. Though Tokyo changes its wardrobe with fickle regularity, it is always careful to adorn itself in jewelry of written words. A logophilic city, in love with words, Tokyo is wrapped, at times sloppily, at other times beautifully or offensively and even absurdly, in words, like a special, well-considered gift.

Singing in the Rainy Season

The first day of rainy season is never the day announced in the paper. The real first day is when the humidity edges over 100 percent, commuters sweat like beer bottles in the sun, umbrellas drip all over the floor, and the morning train stops between stations. Then, the realization that one is trapped, once again, in rainy season condenses in the conscious mind like a sudden downpour.

From then, rainy season takes over all details of life. Shoes become heavy and sullen, as if unwilling to walk, but all too ready to slip on wet patches. Pant cuffs, socks, and the edge of shoulders and bags, all cling like extra, unwanted layers of skin. The whole house turns into a science experiment: shoes become Petri dishes, tile becomes fertile ground, and surfaces reveal their potential for growing new varieties of mold.

Normally rather careful about appearances, in rainy season, Tokyoites carry a ridiculous array of silly-looking towels. They hold these in their hands and try, vainly, to dry themselves. Dignified salarymen wipe their necks with Hello Kitty handkerchiefs. Housewives dab their children's faces with free toy promotion cloths. Young women dab their skin with *omiyage onsen* souvenir hot springs bath towels. In rainy season, appearances just don't matter as much.

Umbrellas become like bodily appendages. If you forget yours, you have to get another, like a lizard growing a new tail. Strangely, though, in a city where every item can be given a high-tech makeover or designer brand marketing, umbrellas remain bland and dull. Few people feel embarrassed to march beneath a 500-yen convenience store umbrella, no matter how expensive their clothes. The rain falls on the expensive and the cheap alike.

Of course, everyone tries to resist at first. Rainy season demands an arsenal of tricks: drying powders, water-pulling tubs, closet dehumidifiers, jacket and coat covers, and special futon storage bags. Every household item is available in a special "anti-mold" version. These measures all sort of work, but not really. Rainy season gets into even the most hidden, interior recesses. No place stays dry.

Rainy season works its way into the emotional interiors, too, transforming Tokyoites into "rainy season personality." The overexposure to humidity and grayness effects a personality change from passive equanimity to open complaint and demonstrative suffering. Tokyoites glance skyward and calculate with obvious self-pity just how wet they are likely to get. With their "rainy season faces" on, Tokyoites wince and shake their heads. Audible groans, aggressive frowns and peevish looks contest against the sound of falling rain.

Then, sometime after days and weeks of rain, another aesthetic takes over altogether. The tempo of life slows down and people become differently aware of their surroundings. Tokyoites start to step nimbly, no longer aggressively jousting with their umbrellas. They set aside their brash forward-leaning approach to life and consider the rain. In short, Tokyoites are humbled by rainy season. They submit. Their pride dissolves.

Then, after accommodating themselves to its omnipresence, what appears to the new rainy season senses are rich variations of grey, amazing rivulets of raindrops, diamond patterns of lights, fluctuating cool breezes and the gentle swooshing of tires. Umbrellas turn the sidewalks into a pumping carousel of colored half-spheres. Everyone sways like jugglers in a huge rainy parade, marching through the city like children.

Coming home turns into a special pleasure. *"Tadaima"* ("I'm home") is inflected to mean "I made it!" The *genkan*, like a castle moat, becomes the site of last resistance. Everything from wet shoes to dripping umbrellas, used cans of waterproof spray, rags for wiping the bicycle seat, torn leaves, and drowned bugs all accumulate there without quite making it all the way inside. Crossing the *genkan*, a wistful calm takes over as the rain pours down outside, and you are suddenly almost dry.

In a city like Tokyo, where the artificial looms over every centimeter and moment of life, the rainy season humbles everyone down to the same watery level. Rainy season is a forced meditation on nature's power to affect us humans in ways that we only half-understand and only partially admit. The rain calls us back to ourselves. No matter how magnificent or extraordinary their cities become, humans remain always, after all, mostly water. Rainy season reminds us that we are closer to the rain than we are to the concrete.

Part Five
A Maze of the Mind

Up and Down and Down and Up– City of Stairs

One day soon after I first moved to Tokyo, a woman in front of me raced down a flight of station stairs too quickly. On the way down, she somehow stepped wrongly on one of her high heels and tumbled forward, her body cartwheeling a couple of steps before landing hard right on her butt. As she went down, one hand grasped for the rail as both her shoes went flying off her feet, embarrassing her first by falling down and second by losing her shoes. She was not hurt, but as she stood up smoothing her tight skirt, the first thing she did was to turn back up the steps to the crowd behind her and say with a bow, "*Sumimasen. Gomen nasai.*"

Her tumble right in front of me was a good warning. On the stairways of Tokyo, one moves up and down at one's own peril. Since then, I have always tried to be careful on Tokyo's omnipresent stairs. Still, I have stumbled, tripped, mis-stepped and once, when drunk in Shibuya, even tumbled down the city's stairs. I finally have come to realize that the most common *kanji* in the city are "*ue*"

Beauty and Chaos

and "*shita*," up and down.

Tokyo is a city of stairs. All through the city, stairs connect different levels and offer footsteps to a populace that is constantly in not only forward motion, but also upwards and downwards as well. Stairs connect different planes of ground, levels in buildings, sections of stores, floors, half-floors and step-ups, off-angles of mismatched sidewalks and obvious mistakes in urban planning.

The city is glued together with a vast and bewildering array of different-sized, different-purposed stairs. There are more different kind of stairs here than any city in the world. Reflecting the way the city was built, torn down, rebuilt and constantly fiddled with, these stairs are a testament to how difficult it is to get it all to fit together. Other cities of the world, built on hills, have a kind of uniformity to their stairs, whether ancient or modern. Tokyo's stairs are a mishmash.

Stairs arch up small hills, cascade down the side of small parks and speckle the urban outdoors. Metal stairs are welded onto the back of buildings and run up and over busy intersections like *torii*. Circular stairs spiral up the middle of teensy stores and thick chunks of concrete march up big front doors. Some stairs fit long leg-lifts while others force everyone to mince up and down like ballerinas. One two-floor house I lived in had stairs so sharply vertical you had to climb them like a ladder using

Up and Down and Down and Up—City of Stairs

your hands.

Walking in Tokyo is as much like climbing a mountain as strolling a river valley. The up and down of it all can be tiring not only because of the expended energy but because one always has to pay attention to unexpected steps and stairs. It is often said that Tokyo women's legs have such beautiful shape because of all the walking they do, and few people in Tokyo have undeveloped calf muscles.

Even a simple train change can involve hundreds of steps, so commuters plan their commutes around station escalators and elevators. The special stair-climbing machine used to haul magazines and drinks up the station steps to kiosks is one of the most sensible inventions I've seen—a constant aggravation, a perfect solution. I'd like to have one myself.

The etiquette of moving to the left side when taking an escalator so that others can walk faster up the right is hardly ever followed on stairs. Stairs remain a site of uncompromising struggle. On crowded stairways, everyone seems to purposely disregard the arrows and lines trying vainly to direct traffic. People tend to push ahead at any angle and look aggravated if they have to step aside. Like some ancient conflict left unresolved, stairs seem to draw out inner frustrations.

And as with many elements of Tokyo, the symbolic and the practical are intertwined. The up and down-ness of the city is simply a practical response to the number of people, but contains a cultural conception of verticality. Tokyo just has to go up and down to fit everyone in and let them all move, but beyond that, stairs become metaphors for the struggle of upward and downward position.

Even little teensy steps mark symbolic space. Stepping down from a room, up to the tile of a toilet, down from the porch or up at a *genkan* are important transformations. One acts, feels and thinks a little differently after moving from one level of space to the other. The inner and outer boundaries are demarcated by a stair, like the level of where heads are when bowing politely. Height is an important marker of meaning, just as the verbs *agaru* and *sagaru*, ascend and descend, are essential to the language. The gods at temples, of course, are always up a few wooden stairs.

Stairs reveal the fault lines in Tokyo's urban planning. Everything seems to be either "*agaru*" (moving up) or "*sagaru*" (moving down), though never coherently. Nothing quite fits in Tokyo, as if the stairs perpetually try to re-align the city's levels and get them all to match back up, but finally gave up and became resigned to all the height differences. I love the constant movement of my legs, though it's easy to get tired, the subtle shifts of height, and even the constant monitoring of the sidewalk for little ups or downs.

Up and Down and Down and Up—City of Stairs

That nothing quite fits at the same level seems a marvelous sloppiness. You see people at all levels on stairs, and in the city as well. The unevenness of Tokyo, physically and socially, is one of its most intriguing and endearing features, and one that Tokyoites experience with plenty of ups and downs.

A-maze-ing Tokyo

Tokyo is a maze within a maze, ad infinitum. The manifold patterns of the city, from the largest overarching structures to the smallest cellular spaces, combine into elaborate and unsymmetrical overlapping mazes. From any single point, you will always be entangled in multiply embedded mazes, some of which are not even apparent. Tokyo's labyrinthine meta-structure repeats itself everywhere, from the twist and turn of narrow alleys to station buildings, magazine layout pages, and the tangled, layered, thinking and feeling of the people.

In store interiors, for example, the winding tangle of aisles, shelves and walls presents goods and products so that you can never see too many things at once. Though grocery stores and other western-style stores rely on linearity and symmetry, most stores drag you into and around their tricky design with subtle spatial clues and visual teases. You feel lost, then found, over and over, until the befuddled amusement and suspicion of being somehow fooled with induces a kind of accepting, playful mind-set.

Stores are laid out like deviously contrived funhouses

offering goods while demanding self-propelled motion through visual contrivances and spatial dividers. Even small boutiques have little handwritten maps and markers to guide you through with suggestive hints. More obvious are the crowd control markers of large, perplexing train stations. They force you to run through the station's maze by a commanding series of arrows, signs, and markers. Stations guide you in and out efficiently, but stores guide you around and around not towards what you want or need so much as what you did not even know existed. The west has window-shopping; Tokyo has maze-shopping.

It took me a long time to get used to seeing details in focus, then seeing a limited section, while always being denied a total view. I got lost constantly. I rambled around stations, mistook directions, forgot locations and generally wandered with a prideful, unhelpful logicality. Now, the main thing I always remind myself when trapped inside is to keep moving and not look too closely. To survive without exhaustion in Tokyo, I gradually trained myself to feel comfortable with moving forward and backward, feeling lost and then found, getting stuck and then breezing on. In America, life moves in forward-looking, straight trajectories. The first years living in Tokyo I felt like my smooth, flat, linear ability to walk and look was constantly being crumpled up like a piece of paper.

The visual field of Tokyo is wrinkled into smaller bits

A-maze-ing Tokyo

and pieces than I had ever been used to, or even imagined, as if contained and directed by a very narrow camera lens. Through the lens, only certain things can be seen, while others remain always outside the frame. Like the rules of a game, these visual and spatial restrictions give pleasure through the alternating condition of being totally lost and then feeling proud to have found the way out. Tokyo's where-the-hell-am-I confusion unfolds into the amusement of finally figuring out exactly where you are. You always know you'll get out of a particular maze, but you never know when.

It took me a long time to notice how lost everyone else is as well. Tokyoites also stumble around blocks and buildings trying to find the right entrance; or get halfway out exits only to suddenly turn around and head back in another direction; and chronically consult maps in the hope of being guided past the detours, dead ends and indirections of the city. One of the primary purposes of cellphones is to rescue hopelessly lost friends and guide them safely by voice to the right place. The answer to the ritual cellphone question, "Where are you now?" is never that easy to truly know, but through question and answer ("What can you see now? And now? Did you pass the stoplight?"), the maze can be solved as a group project.

All this confusion produces a peculiar and distinctive Tokyo mindset—patient reception. Compared to me,

Beauty and Chaos

Tokyoites move around swimmingly with this type of spatial ambiguity. They spend their entire lives somewhere in some maze; so can wait impassively for the next direction and next view. To become impatient is pointless, since nothing will be revealed until you get to the right standpoint. To look, walk and wait is usually rewarded, though not always predictably, and easy to shrug off when not rewarded. After living in Tokyo, I have gradually accustomed myself to this maze mindset, but for Tokyoites, it seems as natural as breathing.

This maze-mind has spiritual roots in Japanese tradition. Classical garden construction, the most famous example being Ryoanji in Kyoto, is made of fifteen stones placed so that from nowhere can all be seen at once. This contrived refusal of the total view is inspired by Zen, and offers the chance to contemplate a microcosm of experience. No two people can ever see the same exact view of the rock garden. All is relative. The practical application of this principle to daily Japanese life can be found everywhere from homes to shopping areas, restaurants and neighborhood streets, only with a lot less enlightenment.

And like other Buddhist teachings, the lesson feels better when wrapped in beauty. Tokyo's maze on maze is like a kimono, which is, after all, a maze of clothing. The beauty of the city comes from not quite being able to see all its colors and patterns at once. You have to roam your eye

A-maze-ing Tokyo

all over a kimono, and over Tokyo, to enjoy the separate sections without ever quite capturing a complete holistic sense. Some part always remains tantalizingly unseen. Like the confusing tangles of beautiful disconnection in a dream, Tokyo's mazes achieve a choppy, baffling kind of flow, but flow nonetheless. It is no coincidence that the word "maze" and "amazed" have the same linguistic root. Tokyo's mazes create a constant state of a-maze-ment.

The Shiny and the Rough

Tokyo's dual nature, traditional and ultra-modern is often noted, but I think the city divides according to its surfaces. The modern part of Tokyo is covered in mirrors, shiny glass, polished chrome, and windows that create fragments of reflections, caught images, and bright glare. The inverse of that are the dark exteriors of traditional Japanese buildings and residential areas. This "flat" non-reflecting side of Tokyo is calmer, plainer and somehow more humble. These areas have natural or wood colors that soak up light and give a single image, rather than reflecting everything back in reverse.

Tokyo can be divided into shiny and flat, but of course, it's not always clearly separated. My gaze feels alternately absorbed, by flat colors, or thrown back, by shiny surfaces. Often this happens in the same visual frame, when the polished gleam of a fast food shop, for example, glares out next to the subdued wooden planks fronting a *ramen* shop. The back and forth between the two can be dizzying, but contributes to Tokyo's oddly variegated visual charm.

From my home to the station, the first few residential streets have only neutral, natural colors. Trees, bushes, hushed house colors, grey walls and brown fencing are punctuated only by mirrors set at cross streets to see passing cars and a few cleanly polished vending machines standing in pairs.

Closer to the station, though, the balance shifts. The subdued colors become gradually replaced by shinier surfaces that reflect my image as I pedal past. Video stores, pachinko parlors, drug and cosmetic stores are all shiny surface operations. I begin to see myself closer up in the bank windows, no doubt wiped and squeegeed that morning. The automatic doors of the convenience stores, having caught me in their sensors, open up and split my image in two.

The station's plastic walls reflect the light pouring from the banks of overhead lights. The floor, though covered in grime and dust, still manages to catch the glint of the overhead bulbs. The ticket machine glass shoots back a ghostly image of myself. A mirror below an advertisement and above a small trashcan is wide enough for two people to check their outfits at a time. Two large gleaming pillars on either side of the platform kiosk pull my reflection into a cylindrical joke shape and then release it.

The train windows are almost entirely covered in reflections. Only by squeezing next to the door window can you see out without catching the image of other passengers. The bright interior has chrome railings and baggage shelves that play with the incoming daylight. Advertisements are so clean and glossy they catch slivers of light from all directions. Outside, the passing windows of office buildings catch the sky, street and train and bounce them back in angled images. Farther into the city, many buildings are entirely designed with the reflections of surrounding buildings in mind.

Mirrors are placed everywhere, like some sort of comic reality television screen. In Tokyo, you see yourself all day long. Or rather, you see bits and pieces of yourself reflected back in all these surfaces. People stop constantly in bathrooms, station platforms and wherever else to check themselves out in what must be a huge industry of mirrors. The mirror on the outside of a photo booth finds a girl checking her bangs. And for those people who don't trust there to be a mirror almost always at hand, they carry their own, furtively checking their look while sitting on the train, relaxing into a seat or waiting for a friend.

The vanity of the city exposes itself in these omnipresent reflections, but the effect is that Tokyo becomes a city of dual motion, dual location, and dual existence. Visually, this constant reflection of shiny surfaces creates an illusion of more space than really exists. Without these illusory shiny surfaces, Tokyo would appear infinitely smaller and chokingly claustrophobic. The shininess also enhances the sense of constant motion. People move twice, it seems, with every motion occurring in reverse on some surface. This dislocating "twinning" of images makes Tokyo appear to be double the size and double the tempo.

Tokyo can be very disturbing with all its mirroring chrome and glass surfaces. At times, it's exciting, like stepping into a game center, but at other times, it gives me a kind of motion sickness. Few other cities put such a visual strain on the peripheral vision of its inhabitants. Tokyo's surfaces define the atmosphere, feeling and character of different areas, and it's fascinating to have such a complex texture of interwoven aesthetic tendencies, which are less in competition perhaps than complementary.

For me, part of the pleasure of getting back home to the darker, natural colors of my neighborhood and home is to not have something shining in my eyes at last. After trouncing through the city of reflections everyday, I feel, on returning home, like I'm stepping back out of the mirror in "Alice Through the Looking Glass." I can almost hear a cartoon "pop" as my reflected images coalesce back into the singularity of who I am at home and I can look straight at objects without seeing them looking back.

Escalators to Heaven

Whenever I shop in Tokyo, I stand amazed on the tremendous sets of escalators running through department stores like some gigantic silver spinal cord. Tokyo is filled with escalators; from the most superfluous meter-high midgets to whopping three-story monsters snaking down the deepest subway stations and specially designed ones that handle luggage carts along with jetlagged humans at Narita airport.

More and more escalators are taking over the stairs of Tokyo. The designs adapt to different spaces: one-person wide escalators in tight exits; brief flat slidewalk sections that then curve back up; innovative handicapped access attachments; and sensor-driven ones that run or reverse only when a human arrives. The continued evolution of escalator technology shows how deeply ingrained they have become as a major mode of transportation.

The appeal of escalators is their comfort. Gone are the people in your way and ahead only open space as you stand contentedly pulled along by the power of a machine. The soothing pace (no doubt carefully researched by some company), the cleanliness (since escalators are polished to a shine by teams of cleaners), and the acquiescent effortlessness (so different from jockeying through crowds or rocking unbalanced on the train) make me feel like I'm very nearly flying, at least compared to the rest of Tokyo's transport.

In many places, as you ride you can stare openly at streams of people you'll never ever see again. Clear dividers allow you to gaze out over the momentary succession of landings, shopping areas and passing environments. The feeling of motion and the view of people and places is what make escalators more fun than the dull tube-like experience of elevators. Escalators are a bit of Disneyland compared to the closed cells of elevators.

On escalators, I always feel like I am floating upwards like a feather. The gentle motion, the massaging rhythm, the subtle hum of gears, lulls me like a baby in a crib. I can appreciate the entirely planned and neatly executed environment I survey. Like other "escalatees," I relax into the flow and unwind. To be on an escalator is to be surrounded by artificial clouds of displays bathed in soft lighting. You merge into the environment in the way you do from a mountaintop view. In this sense, escalators are seductive.

The effect can be profound, though mostly unconscious. On any one day, an average Tokyoite will ride many escalators. The numerous escalators subtly shift

Escalators to Heaven

the psychological framework. Escalators are like walking without walking, anesthetizing the loco-motor part of the brain that normally works overtime in Tokyo. Escalators speed up the process of becoming pacified, mesmerized, and ready to accept whatever is next.

In that sense, the escalator is the insulating and comforting entryway to the consumer psychology, with its constant whispering drone, "Let me walk for you, let me climb for you, let me take you to heaven." Rather than promising constituents more highways, politicians could probably garner more votes by promising more escalators.

Besides their simple convenience, Tokyo escalators have an element of social etiquette to them. One of the most-followed public rules in Tokyo is stepping to the left on an escalator. Well-dressed businessmen step aside for high school students, young *fureeta* apologize to lively, retired people, as everyone respects the right to walk faster on the right hand side. It's pleasant to relax on the left while others rush frantically past; but it's equally pleasant to pass everyone by and feel like you're getting ahead on the right.

But more than that, escalators are in and of themselves polite. Not only because of the graying of the population, but as an act of social consideration, escalators are a kind of welcome mat into the spaces of Tokyo. To NOT have an escalator is kind of impolite; and to have one enters the riders into a web of obligations. It's not that you HAVE to buy something after riding, it's that you feel more like buying something if you are comfortable and not tired.

Escalators pull you up and into a new space quickly and discreetly. Just like at the *genkan* to any house, where "*agatte kudasai*" welcomes you to the interior space, escalators simply transport you up and in, or down and in, as the case may be, with silent politeness. Each rising or lowering on an escalator is also an entering, not only at department stores, but also into a new station, a new train line, a new building, or some newly defined and directed area. Escalators work as the polite, mechanical entryway to thousands of spaces all through the city.

I wonder whether in the future escalators will replace all stairs in Tokyo. It's easy to become addicted to technology and it's almost a shock when one breaks down and you have to walk against your will. I wonder what it would mean to have a city with no stairs, where all rising and falling is mechanically propelled. Though a great convenience, escalators make it easy to be acquiescent and inactive. Regardless of whether one wants more exercise or opposes wasteful energy consumption, one of Tokyo's central dynamics is this constant push and pull between the comfortingly mechanical and the exhaustingly human.

The Love of Small Places

"It's so teensy I'm not sure I can find it again."

"You hardly notice it walking by."

"I found it by chance, but I'll have to take you there."

"It's just a small, little place."

"You can only just squeeze in a few people."

Among the highest compliments one can give a place in Tokyo are ones like the above. Though the vast scale of Tokyo keeps expanding in all directions, the contained compact space of little interiors still thrives. Though haiku, bonsai and other miniature arts have long been accorded cultural respect, the incredible, small interiors of Tokyo's shops and restaurants deserve as much recognition. These small interiors are brilliantly alive, and an essential aspect of the city.

Clubs, eateries, stalls, and boutiques abound in the nooks and crannies of a city that at first glance appears to be spreading awkwardly and unconsciously without plan. The outside surfaces of Tokyo often feel sloppy and indifferent, as if thrown up any old way. Small in Tokyo feels very different. The contrast between the huge, sprawling exterior and the simple purposive interiors could hardly

Beauty and Chaos

be stronger. These little insides feel honest and natural, well designed and womb-like—the inverse compensation for Tokyo's outsides.

Smallness, a general Japanese obsession, ensures that the human element is not lost, a safeguard against the vanity of large, depersonalized perspectives. In small places you *have to* talk with people. The small size of a place, whether for food, clothing, or specialty goods, guarantees quality. Large places tend to hedge their bets against large rents by dispensing the predictably commercial, the easy moneymaker. They cater to the insecure. Small places invite the culturally and urbanely confident.

This association of smallness with quality comes out of a well developed and flourishing tradition of craft. The attention to detail at the core of craft is hard to produce consistently in large places, where tasks are divided and isolated as if on a factory assembly line, so that they lose the handmade feeling. In the craft tradition, one person handles one step at a time with singular care, knowing the entire process. Small places continue the tradition of personal, individual mastery, no matter what they offer.

Small places have a view of motion and space that relies on practiced efficiency and acquired skill. No motion is wasted, but all are smooth, confident and aesthetically pleasing in themselves. The thrust of the knife, the handing over of an item, even the placement of plates, glasses

The Love of Small Places

or bottles is well considered yet performed without over-attention to form. The atmosphere derives from an interactive sense of space rather than from a contrived video game-like escape. The small size brings people together rather than separating and isolating them.

Time becomes human-oriented. Dishes are not handed over when finished in some distant kitchen, but the delivery is timed by watching the customers to see when they are ready. The external Tokyo sense of urgency is, like a well-cooked fish, thereby de-boned. The outside world's demands and concerns feel pushed aside to focus on the moment and its pleasures. They relax.

Entering a small space means entering its unique flow and being part of it. From the moment one steps inside a small eating spot, the "master" is looking around, imagining what kind and how many dishes the entering customer will order, recalculating how energy must be redistributed and how the entire space will best accommodate the people there. Actions are nonchalantly narrowed and naturally focused.

A customer is not there regardless, and is not interchangeable, but creates a unique ripple in the organic flow of people, objects and energy. In a small place, individuals matter. Outside in Tokyo, individuality tends to be lost in its sheer massive scale. Any scene outside would be the same regardless of whether you are there or not.

Beauty and Chaos

Small spaces rely on an intuitive sense of being in the same space. They demand an attention to other people based on feeling and care.

Of course, that dwarfing unpredictability and immense scope makes the outside of Tokyo its own kind of anonymous pleasure. Inside, the intensity is like a traditional tea ceremony room; outside, the intensity comes from the open, swirling chaos of it all. Ultimately, though, the two work together. The small spaces of Tokyo create a cellular vitality that is the essential counterpart of its overarching chaos and confusion. Tokyo's small interiors resuscitate its inhabitants and bring its overwhelming size down to a human scale.

Around and Around–Going in Circles

On a recent trip to Beijing and Shanghai, I found myself comforted by the surroundings. After living in Tokyo, the long stretches of unbending roads, sharp-angled turns and broad, open views of Chinese cities made me feel, strangely, like I was somehow home in an American city. In Beijing and Shanghai, like New York and American cities, you can always head straight ahead towards your goal and see right where you're going.

In Tokyo, though, going straight ahead means you'll smack into something. You can ONLY get anywhere in Tokyo by meandering around. In Tokyo, I always feel like I'm running around in circles—literally. Veering lines gently guide you in curving, roundabout directions. It's hard to find a perfectly straight road or view anywhere. Every city has its own favorite shapes that repeat over and over in endless variations and Tokyo's basic urban building block is not a block at all, but a circle.

Tokyo's twisting and turning circularity gives me a kind of seasickness. I find myself bobbing and weaving

Beauty and Chaos

through crowds, careening around corners, and trying to keep my balance. The whole city moves in curves as if straight rulers had never been invented and instead the city was drawn only with the circling sweep of protractors and compasses.

At the heart of Tokyo is a circle. The Yamanote line is not a perfect circle, it's more of a scrunched-up egg, but it certainly isn't rectangular. Inside that is the Emperor's palace, and outside the Yamanote spin train lines that look like the rays from a child's drawing of the sun.

This circuitous branching out shape repeats all over. The front areas of most train stations have a circle for taxis and buses, then another circle of convenient shops—*ramen*, groceries, coffee shops, and drug stores. The streets wander off in all directions from the center like spider webs. In the morning rush hour, people converge on the station from 360 degrees, finally, becoming linearized only once inside the train.

Neighborhoods, too, defy linearity. The numbering of houses refers not to a point on a line, but to a vague area somewhere on a roundabout shape. In New York, an address like "98 west 45th Street" takes you in two straight lines from wherever you are right to a single point. Numbers and names in Tokyo tend to indicate undefined areas, "*nani-nani-mae*," in front of that place, rather than precise points. To get anywhere in Tokyo, you have to use a kind

Around and Around—Going in Circles

of fuzzy logic, a swirling, back-and-forth way of thinking that excludes specificity and linearity.

As a result, more often than not, Tokyo has only partial views. You can't see around a circle after all. Straight, long, direct views can be had only from the highest skyscrapers; at street level sidewalks are not wide enough and streets too jammed to get perspective. Western cities are built with symbolic views and open symmetry. Compared to the west, Tokyo rarely offers a huge clear view of the entire front of a building or the entire expanse of a boulevard. The view is always deterred by curves.

A circular feeling too molds interiors. *Depachika* department store basements, for example, feel like merry-go-rounds of food stalls. I find myself walking around and around inside them, passing by the same fish, miso or cake counter again and again. Department stores, too, direct the shopper, setting up walking paths for shopping circulation.

Every culture has essential shapes that mold the external shapes. These develop primarily in response to the natural environment. Japan's natural geography allows few straight lines amid the rivers, mountains and forests. In America, Australia or Africa, in contrast, straight lines are easy to follow with the eye across vast plains.

These circles also manifest in Japan's spiritual life. Japanese pilgrimages, whether in Kyushu or *shitamachi*, involve walking around and around a circling route of temples. Western pilgrimages are pretty much straight lines right up to the holy spot and then straight back home. Monks silently meditate by walking in circles around Mount Hiei to achieve enlightenment, and Tokyo is not so different.

The effect of all this is powerful. It shapes how one experiences the environment, and consequently how one thinks and feels. In Tokyo, for me, there is a kind of vertigo, but also a softness and comfort in all these rounded edges and curved spaces. Tokyo's little daily pilgrimages are ones that circle around back to their starting point—enlightenment or not.

Bonsai Buildings

Tokyo's urban landscape is an architectural struggle. Throughout the city, post-war 90-degree angles tussle with pre-modern curves and ancient lines. Tokyo's urban design seems to be evolving, sadly, towards more imposing and more conventional schemes, so it is always a pleasure to come across intriguing pockets of quirky disruption. While new mansions, gray skyscrapers and multi-floored pachinko parlors square up ever-bigger sections of Tokyo, weird-shaped pockets of leftover land squeeze in unique architectural gems.

The wonder of these quirky, odd-shaped buildings is how they can wedge themselves into such compact spaces. Near where I live is perhaps the thinnest building in Tokyo, an arm-span-wide triangle of a building that stretches alongside a slope above a train track. In any other city in the world, the space would just be left vacant. Every time I pass, I marvel at how they have finagled just enough room from the ever-expanding grid of so-called progress to make, with child-like confidence, a space to live. Walking through Tokyo's neighborhoods, I always delight in stumbling across one of these strange

Beauty and Chaos

little buildings snuggled into the most unlikely nooks and crannies.

In some places in Tokyo, the designs of these buildings fall into sleek parallelograms or snipped-off pentangles, molded up from the city's complex jigsaw puzzle of land. In between Y-shaped roads or at the edges of *chome*, the oddly shaped equivalents to "blocks" of city space, are endlessly arrayed cleverly cast walls. As much sculpture as construction, these walls take the irregularity of the land below and project it several floors higher. Where widened roads chop open dense neighborhoods or train lines slice into traditional shopping districts, these little buildings hunker slyly among the mass-produced mansions and bland office complexes that loom over them like architectural bullies.

In its rush to modernity, Tokyo is becoming molded too much by easy math. Most new buildings are easy to measure, design, and build, but very dull to contemplate. Urban designers now try to square things up. Even when postmodern buildings juggle shapes, they sometimes try too hard, and end up imposing their professional creativity unnaturally. These smaller odd-shaped buildings, in contrast, feel organic and needed, as if they have sprouted from human conditions and belong on their own terms. By confounding conventional geometry, their eccentric charm seems more of a humble reply to the question of

Bonsai Buildings

space than a conquest.

Though seemingly an afterthought, these odd-shaped buildings form an integral part of the urban layout. When walking through the endless series of big-box buildings that now dominate most neighborhoods, they have an impact far beyond their size. Like the single small stone in a rock garden set alone at a distance, they balance out the central heavy configuration and give it character. Like bonsai, they rest in a constricted base and flourish in pleasing asymmetric shapes.

These buildings are not just making a virtue of necessity. They go beyond reluctant practicality into an innovative aesthetic that revels in gorgeous irregularity. Their way of working within strict limitations and cleverly resolving problems of design also reveals an earthy humor. While the rest of Tokyo's buildings scowl and frown, they smile amused at themselves.

When I walk past one, I always stop and wonder if the architect, working feverishly with protractor, triangle and stencils, laughed at the bizarre blueprints. I can picture the builders smugly pleased at the tightness of the final fit, delighted at rightly measuring the erroneous mis-measure. You can sense the pleasure the shaping involved, the careful constructing that demanded tools capable of many degrees other than 90. It is not a laugh-out-loud funny, but an ongoing, eye-wrinkling bemusement.

Beauty and Chaos

I can't imagine, though, what it must be like to live inside such different shapes and angles. Do the inhabitants have to pare down their bookshelves or doors to fill the on-rectangular space? Do they eat breakfast on a rhom-boid table and shower in a parallelogram? Do they hang winter coats at the large end of their triangular closets and belts at the pointed end? I feel envious of their freedom from conventional 90-degree experience. I, too, would like to try out new shapes, to immerse myself in peculiar geometry, to be surrounded by wry forms that might make even my thoughts re-form themselves into new patterns.

I also wonder about the histories of the unusual shapes of land, how they were divided, drafted and re-drawn over the years. A time-lapse video capturing the decades of suc-cessive buildings rising and falling on these spatial para-doxes would be fascinating. What past odd eyes cut them up like this? What necessities of life, arguments over boundary lines, or generational splits cut and re-cut these shapes. Of course, no such history is possible, since Tokyo keeps flowing towards the future by erasing the inconve-niences of the past with a quick sleight of hand. These bonsai buildings write a human history not of words but of form.

What I like best about these buildings is their resistance to the general trend towards convenience, common sense and ordered predictability. Tokyo too often takes

Bonsai Buildings

the easy way out and rebuilds itself into the ordinary and unexceptional. Bonsai buildings defy that trend. In the fiercely contested drama of Tokyo's confining spaces, where towering structures vault upward and outward in spatial conquest, these intriguing weird-angled designs signal a persistent vitality in thinking and living. They testify to the ongoing creative and quirkily human response that adapts to the past, and to reality, by adding zest to the present.

Part Six
After Words

Seeing the City, Reading the City

Most people respond very little to their environment. They do not notice details or examine what is in front of them. They react unconsciously, I am sure, but often do not consciously articulate what they see. Whether we ignore it or not, at an unconscious level, meaning is always at work in the gigantic city we live inside. This looking-away is part of the Tokyo attitude to life, and while that's fine for others, it's not an attitude I share. Socrates said, "the unexamined life is not worth living," and I would add that the unexamined city is not worth living in.

Reading Tokyo has become an important part of my life. By "reading" I mean Tokyo is as complex as a long novel, as confusing as an avant-garde film and, sometimes, as strikingly beautiful as calligraphy. As a foreigner living in this city, many patterns startle and amuse me that Japanese friends do not even notice. I look at Tokyo with not only foreign eyes but also small town eyes. Those are the only eyes I have. These too-familiar aspects are often the richest in meaning and reveal the interior complexity of the city.

The American writer Henry David Thoreau in "On

Beauty and Chaos

Walden Pond" stated his reasons for living in the woods and writing about it very clearly 200 years ago. He wrote, "I went to the woods because I wished to live deliberately, to front only the essential facts of life, and see if I could not learn what it had to teach, and not, when I came to die, discover that I had not lived. I did not wish to live what was not life, living is so dear... I wanted to live deep and suck out all the marrow of life." Though the Massachusetts woods and Tokyo megalopolis differ vastly, his attitude of confronting and learning and writing is one I deeply ad-mire.

Thoreau was not afraid of the results, either. He wrote that if life in the woods "proved to be mean, why then to get the whole and genuine meanness of it, and publish its meanness to the world; or if it were sublime, to know it by experience, and be able to give a true account of it." That is easier said than done, of course, but to keep an open, searching attitude makes life not only more meaningful, but more delightful as well. Curiosity killed the cat, but satisfaction brought him back, is an American saying.

I find living in Tokyo alternately alienating, confusing, and aggravating, yet to balance the "meanness," I look for the sublime. Many people adapt to Tokyo by focusing narrowly on their work, friends, family, vacations and passing pleasures. Letting your sensitivity respond to the environment can be painful and shocking. Tokyo is an over-

Seeing the City, Reading the City

whelming city. But, I did not want to live here and not really live here fully. I want to look at it closely.

I sometimes retreat back to the comfortable interior of university life. It is easy to hide in the routine of writing journal articles about literature, attending meetings (and complaining), and helping students broaden their learning. But I distrust that comfort and safety when it lacks the excitement that comes from confusion and conflict. Concentration on one thing can sometimes be escape from another thing. However, two different wavelengths when in sync make a fuller and stronger resonance. For me, teaching makes me want to write and writing makes me want to teach.

I sometimes dream of moving, too. If I could transplant my life as is to New York or Paris or London, I would consider it seriously. I always loved cities. Paris is a place that I find endlessly fascinating, as is New York, London, Madrid and Beijing (where I spent three years of my life). I lived in Sydney for six months, and have been fascinated by New Orleans, Shanghai, Chengdu, Lhasa, Yogyakarta, Varanasi, Bangkok, Hong Kong, Rome, Istanbul, New Delhi, Calcutta, Jakarta, Copenhagen, San Francisco, Chicago and of course Kyoto. None of them are like Tokyo, though. If I had time, I'd live in those cities, too, and write about them like I have here.

I like small places, and small towns, the countryside

also, but something about big cities seems to really get me. It's hard to define why, but energy is one of the main reasons. In college, when I first started spending time in New York, just hitting the streets there felt like a shot of tequila. Tokyo is an equally intense place, though in very different ways. More than other world cities, Tokyo bubbles over into streams of complex meanings of many different kinds. From small museums like the *bonenkai* museum, to teeny standing bars in Kanda, to the awesome ancient temples, bizarre contemporary architecture and hordes of commuting, consuming humans, Tokyo's supply of meaning-creating challenges is inexhaustible.

Tokyo is hard to see, not only because it presses up close and disallows perspective, but is also hard to connect up, as it stretches over a huge swath of territory, both literal and figurative. In Tokyo, one's gaze is always focused ahead on a single point, with passing details hard to grasp. Much of its life takes place hidden away or in small details, and none of it ever seems to be openly explained. I have to force myself at times to not passively zone out but instead actively look around and try to look inside.

A lot of times, I find it easier to put my eyes in a book, my ears in my ipod, and my body at an indifferent posture. I can understand why so many people immerse themselves in a sharply narrow focus. After a break, though, that passive indifference becomes dull to me, and I start looking

Seeing the City, Reading the City

around again. I consciously search for connections, and take in as much as I can before overloading. I try to let the city wash over me and reveal its secrets in its own magical way. When I do, I'm always eventually rewarded.

The City Provokes Me–Why I Write These

Writing about Japanese culture means stepping across a minefield of personal assumptions, intercultural misunderstandings and a social history of hurt feelings. If you are too critical, you are labeled a Japan basher; too positive and you are a Japanophile. Finding the right balance that naturally expresses what you truly want to say becomes enmeshed in past arguments and the matchless confusions of *nihonjinron* books about Japanese.

Japanophiles, it is assumed, are too soft to resist seduction by the Japanese mindset. Japan-bashers are too logical and insensitive to enter into the Japanese mindset. Bashers hold Japan to rigid, judgmental standards, while lovers apologize out of compliance and sloppy relativism. For the most part, both ends of the nihonjinron spectrum have been trained in Japan studies at universities, been given scholarships by the Japanese or foreign governments and have acquired a vast body of received knowledge, accepted theories and demanding training.

More than anything, these two poles—positive and

negative—reflect Japanese reactions to foreigners writing about their culture. On the one hand, Japanese love to read what foreigners think, whether critical or praising, but on the other hand quickly dismiss insights from foreigners as being "external" to a true "inner" understanding. Misunderstandings are often proudly taken as proof of the myth of cultural uniqueness.

To argue whether Japan is *more* unique is less appealing to me than finding the beguiling details and suggestive meanings of its cumulative charm. I am not sure my writings fit at either extreme. I don't either look down on or look up to Tokyo's unique strain of Japanese culture. I try to look right at it and write directly.

My only real qualifications for writing about Tokyo are passion and curiosity. I think of my writing as a response to the rich untapped veins of underlying meanings in the city's life. Tokyo is what I'd call a "juicy" city, lacking the correct anthropological or urban studies jargon. Flavorful, complex, satisfying, and chewy, like a slice of *chashu* meat in *ramen*, Tokyo drives me not towards well-defended conclusions, but towards open-ended musing and unlikely connections.

My own education is in philosophy, education, literature and film. I draw on a little of each in my writing. Ideas, approaches, situations and images intermingle in these essays, without paying heed to the rigorous pro-

The City Provokes Me—Why I Write These

cedures and prescribed frameworks of journalistic, academic, public policy or nihonjinron writing. Like its sodden, reclaimed and earthquake-prone land, Tokyo offers no easy foundation on which to build a high-rise mansion of meta-narrative. That's OK with me. I'm not interested here in accurate historicism, disciplined research, or watertight theories. I'm interested in answering the myriad questions Tokyo asks me every day.

Tokyo is not much written about in proportion to its immensity and complexity. Paris, London, Shanghai and Bombay, cities equal to Tokyo in size, scope and weight have all inspired a vast body of writing. Maybe Tokyo's dispersed areas, obscure history, inconsistent design and incongruous elements resist analysis more than other cities. But that's just all the more reason to write about it. Tokyo begs to be written about, and yet remains shyly elusive.

So, I have responded in essays, a form of writing which fits Tokyo well, I feel. The pattern of essays, like many of Tokyo's patterns, juggles multiple levels of style, tone and phrasing. The short essay best captures and corrals my experience of Tokyo. More than other forms, short essays can directly express feeling, seeing, sorting out, and ruminating to other people. I feel inspired by the constant surprise of the city, and surprise creates its own style and tone and form.

Beauty and Chaos

In English, the word essay derives from French, where it means something like "trying" or "attempting." The great French writer, Michel de Montaigne, was one of the first to "essay" his ideas on topics in this kind of brief, first person, thinking-out-loud form. I like Montaigne's sense of trying; it has a friendly humility to it that enhances curiosity and expands the sense of fun.

Nihonjinron writing usually provides certain answers, but I am trying more to ponder interesting questions. Essays should probe, question and clarify; they do not have to finalize, conclude or prove. They should open up dialogue; they do not need to pass judgments. I do not think my essays will transform anyone's deepest beliefs about Tokyo, but I hope they will defamiliarize what is close but commonly overlooked. I hope readers can see, together with me, the extraordinary in the ordinary.

I probably have often chosen topics, or aspects of topics, that Japanese might not have thought about much at all. Tokyoites accept many parts of their life deeply and unquestioningly. I'm not trying to give Tokyoites a wake-up call—they seem well aware of the city surrounding them—but to share my particular delight and enthusiasm. I don't think I understand Tokyo better than Tokyoites, or better than *nihonjinron* writers, but I understand things differently. When reading these essays, my hope is people pause and think, "I never thought of it like that," or

The City Provokes Me—Why I Write These

"I look at that all the time but never stopped to consider it," because that's how I felt when writing them.

I think reading and writing are very similar processes, though they are usually thought of as opposites. Paradoxical as it may sound, I read the city by writing. I find meaning mostly as I write. Tokyo's subtleties precipitate into meaning only in words. Without writing, Tokyo would remain intangible and its energy concealed. These essays are both an embrace and a pushing back against a city I find alluring and vital, tough and bewildering.

Why anyone would come to live in Tokyo, observe it and write about it is a pretty good question. The answer is in this collection of articles. But really, the question why do I write about Tokyo should be turned around—why do Tokyoites want to read about their own city? Why does anyone else?

Japan and Me

My first memories of other countries were not so distinct or defined. Asia was an abstract bit of homework, a bunch of words like China, Japan, Viet Nam and India dotting a bright-colored map. Growing up in Kansas City, Kansas made other places seem impossibly far away. Because they were. I loved the open spaces, calm natural environment and easygoing manner of the Midwest, but I always suspected Kansas was one phase of my life and another, somewhere else, would happen eventually.

My father had a box in the attic where he kept a pair of *geta* high wooden sandals, *kanji* flashcards, an Arab headdress and souvenirs from his travels. He had been in the medical service in Kure for a couple years, enlisting to get a scholarship to university in exchange. Playing with my sister and our friends, we loved to throw on the Arab headdress, slip our feet into the geta and parade around the house, the flashcards spilling *kanji* all over the wood floors. That's the earliest memory I have of Japan. I've never worn geta since.

When young I often went to see movies with my father at a local art cinema. The theater showed festivals of movies from different countries and for the Japanese series, they showed "Seven Samurai" and "Yojimbo." I thought those were fantastic, like cowboy movies but with swords. A TV program for kids showed foreign films dubbed in English. One of my favorites was called "Fatty and Skinny" about two Japanese boys, one rich and fat and the other poor and skinny, who had all kinds of troubles. They studied at school, fought with bullies, and had a pet dog just like me.

I did not grow up in a city, but in the suburbs. My mother is an artist, of cityscapes and landscapes, and my father is a psychiatrist, so observing and analyzing, seeing and thinking, were bequeathed to me as part of their way of life. We often had foreign doctors from all over the world, Cuba, India, and Persia over to our home. We kids would race around the house and slow down only when they would set up a screen to show slides of photos from their homelands. I would get drowsy after playing, so the slides clicked by like dream images before being carried upstairs to bed. Part of adult life seemed to take place in other countries.

My family's church in the fashionably liberal 60s encouraged us to know about other religions. One of the journalists at the church had lived and worked all over the world. He organized a world religion class for teenagers that drew on his collection of Buddhist statues, sutra scrolls, Islamic books, prayer shawls and endless photos. Compared to the simple, plain, white interior of my church, Eastern religion seemed unbelievably exotic, sensuous and alluring. What really got me, though, was the incense, which he burned during the class on Japan and China. Wow, what a smell!

At college, I had a crush on a girl from California who lent me a copy of Eugene Herrigel's "Zen in the art of Archery." The lean, poetic power of Zen sharply contrasted with the ponderous ideas and inescapable logic of the analytic philosophy I was majoring in. After working through Kant, Hegel, Heidegger, and Plato, I browsed the Zen section of the library, picking through the works of D.T. Suzuki, Alan Watts, and the poetry of Japan and China in translation. Those books on Zen opened up a new set of values.

My university was great for film studies and I could indulge myself in more Japanese films. Classes in semiotics analyzed Japanese films as particularly rich examples of cinematic creation. Lecturers discussed the filmic language and showings featured the classic films of Yasujiro Ozu, Imamura Shohei, Kenji Mizoguchi, and my old favorite Akira Kurosawa. This was before video and DVD, but with university support, the films shown by the student film society were just a dollar.

After college, many of my classmates went to Europe

for a summer of travel before settling into their careers in the fall. Just to be contrary, I went east, to New Zealand and Australia first, to work, and then to Indonesia, my first Asian country, to travel. I backpacked and worked odd jobs for a couple years, moving through Southeast Asia and the Mediterranean towards Europe. I wanted to keep traveling, and decided to teach English so I could live longer in each country rather than just skim over the surface. In short, I was addicted and had to support my habit.

Graduate school back in Kansas was ironically very Asian. I was the lone American in a department filled with Asian grad students studying for their Master's in English. I made good friends from Japan, Korea, China, Sri Lanka, Thailand, and Africa. I started teaching and tutoring and had students from Arabic countries, South America and Asia. I helped them with trivial things like apartment contracts, driver's licenses and cheap shopping, while they opened up my mind to their countries. The Japanese graduate students in particular liked to party, and though I couldn't join them in mah jong, I could eat, drink and talk.

After I finished my degree, I got a call from a university in China offering me a teaching position, with a contract and a plane ticket. It was hard to say no. I studied a little Chinese in the summer, sold my car, said goodbye to friends, apologized to my family for not settling down in Kansas, and took off for the world again.

Japan and Me

Beijing was amazing. This was the years right before the Tien An Men incident, a time of opening and loosening before the later crackdown. I loved it; though living there under the oppressive system of old-style communism was stifling. I invited my students over to the foreign hotel (simply not done at that time), went out with colleagues (shocking to ordinary Chinese), traveled alone all over the country (which often drew a huge crowd), and settled into the excitement of living and working in a completely different environment.

After two years, though, I decided to move on. I had fallen in love with a fellow English teacher at my school who later followed me to Tokyo and became my wife. But I left her there for a while and went on first to Tokyo alone. I wrote to a Japanese friend from graduate school, who had finished his degree and returned to Tokyo. He invited me to stay with him in Tokyo until I got settled. I arrived at Narita and took the bus to Shinjuku, amazed on the way at the city unfolding before me. He and his girlfriend met me at Shinjuku station and we went out for yakitori and beer, my first meal in Japan, and still one of my favorites.

My friend and I lived together in an apartment that looked out over a shopping street. The pachinko parlor, snack bars, and a local dog (that I dropped water on to shut up) were very noisy, but we could sit on the porch, drink beer and watch everyone walking by. He introduced me to strange Japanese foods, and explained strange Japanese things. I liked the way the *chukka* restaurant, liquor store and other small shops remembered me. Of course, no other foreigners lived there, and I felt a sense of community that didn't exist in America. I found it charming.

I bought novels in translation, Yasunari Kawabata, Soseki Natsumi, Junichiro Tanizaki, Saiichi Maruyama and many others, which I read in huge overstuffed chairs in coffee shops in between teaching English at companies. I had a friend who loved to walk around Tokyo. We would meet in between classes and just walk until we got lost. Then, when class time approached, we'd hop on a bus or look for a subway entrance. We stopped to eat in countertop restaurants, poked around in antique stores and wandered through all kinds of shops around Kanda, Suidobashi, Otemachi, Akasaka and Shinjuku where most of the companies we taught at were located.

Wandering around with curiosity as my guide became a pleasure. Observing, asking, stopping in, wondering, and questioning became part of how I lived here. Though I left again for several years to return to graduate school in America, I came back and have lived here since. I still travel a lot, but not as much. I live here now. Tokyo raised many questions that piled up over the years in my mind like unanswered letters. I think these essays are my attempt to answer those questions, but in doing that, I found new questions that I didn't even know I had.

After Words and Thanks

Thanking people is a skill I improved greatly after coming to Japan, a country where you are often elaborately thanked for small things like pressing an elevator button or throwing your trash away in the right place. Even the train ticket machines bow deeply in thanks. As much as I practice thanking here daily, though, I never get the tone, level or direction correct. I have a lot of people to thank for this book, but I worry I will forget someone, especially since my thank-you list is long.

After writing and collecting these essays, I realize that the view I used to have about writing when I was younger is totally incorrect. The fanciful image of the writer bundled against the cold, struggling beside a candle, dipping a crow-quill pen in the last drop of ink is naïve and romantic. The myth of solitary struggle is just that—a myth. Writers are intimately social beings.

Writers are helped by lots of people in both direct and seemingly small ways. Friends say funny things, students ask unexpected questions, strangers make passing insightful (or idiotic) comments, and colleagues shove ideas around like sumo wrestlers. Any of these might precipitate understanding and a focus to write. Writers are like vultures, picking up scraps of ideas, words and images from wherever they can find them, and then working them over alone, and they are very often alone. But still, writing is a profoundly social process.

I don't like to admit it, but in fact I steal ideas from my students all the time. And steal energy, since my students always seem to have more energy than I do. I am amazed at their hard work and creative insights, so they push me to keep going. I'm supposed to be a role model for them, but they are for me, too. Also, there are few things nicer than a student coming up after class and saying, "Sensei, I read your article!" Thanks, students!

Several other writing projects keep me writing and keep me thinking. One colleague continues to drag me into the world of book publishing and refuses to let me leave. He's been waiting patiently for our next book project until this one is done. Talk to you soon, man. I also write about jazz for the Japan Times and write for and edit Jazznin, a bilingual jazz magazine. In this day and age, jazz seems like ancient history to some, so it's surprising any publisher would actually open their pages to an obscure musical style. Writing there keeps me crisp and keeps up my chops. Thanks, jazz-friendly publications and jazz readers!

Most of all, editors are immensely helpful. The editors

at Newsweek magazine, a publication dedicated to bridging the information gap between east and west, invited me to write about Tokyo. They really encouraged me to write from my point of view. Those editors and translators there are excellent. Their emails, along with letters from readers, give me the regular motivation and regular deadlines that keep the flow of writing going. The producers of "Shiten Ronten" at NHK read those Newsweek articles and invited me to speak on their program—unedited. Other producers from Nihon TV and another section of NHK also invited me to video-ize the essays here, and seem to keep inviting me. Thanks, media folks!

The editors of this book read those Newsweek articles and wrote me a wonderful handwritten letter (that I could barely read it was so elegant!) asking me to publish with them. Little did they know I'm not really a Japan specialist, and not good at the language, but am just a literature teacher and jazz maniac. They probably didn't realize how much trouble I'd be, either, but well, too late now. Sorry to fool you guys, but glad I did. As we say in America, "That's very, very cool!"

The suspicion that editors hamper writers or redirect writing how they want it has certainly not been my experience. Editing is a tricky job that handles writer's egos as much as words. Writers love to be taken out to eat and drink by their editors (hint, hint!) and seize on small compliments that they later magnify in importance privately to themselves. "Edit" usually sounds like "cut," but that's the least of it. Editing is directing, suggesting, talking and listening. It's also going to a lot of long, tedious meetings on the writer's behalf. There's no greater sacrifice than meetings.

Those editors have helped me understand, without crushing my spirit, how to get words, and groups of words, to work. Words and ideas can be very clunky and inert at times, always threatening to die on you. Good editors like mine know how to resuscitate my words, my ideas and my enthusiasm. Most importantly, my editors understood my writing. Being understood in that way is a rare thing, and when combined with constructive support, it is unbelievably rare. Thank you very much!

To move meanings from one to another social, cultural and semantic system would seem, at times, an impossible task. Translators must have tremendous facility with two language systems, a love of reading, a mixed bag of linguistic tricks and plenty of intuition. What amazes me is the ability to read and write with such attention to the depth and breadth of intention, implication and feeling. It is a deeply human undertaking, and having found the right translator, I feel I have found a friend.

Note on the translation: Those Japanese readers who have the Japanese version might find differences between the versions.

After Words and Thanks

It's the writing, not the translating. The translators did an excellent job; it's me that changed things. As the language ping-pongs back and forth, new ideas arise, and the essays change. Sorry they're not exactly the same always!

Writing in one language, English, and being translated into another, Japanese, feels a little like talking through a screen, like women did in ancient Heian Kyoto. Though I can read and speak Japanese, I cannot write well in it. I wrote these essays all in English originally. My translator for the original version has captured the spirit as well as the letter of my writing, and that is really the highest compliment to be paid to any translator. I feel lucky to have found such a sensitive and talented person. Thank you in both languages!

Being married to a writer is a drag. It's a lot of getting out of the way, usually when you least want to. Writing involves putting yourself in a neurotic, introverted state of mind that is hard to get back out of. It's a selfish activity that is highly addictive. Like martial arts, it's designed to hurt someone, but doesn't have to. Writing inevitably drains energy from the rest of your life. However, writing makes life deeply meaningful and wildly interesting. A house packed with ideas, words, and books is the best place to live. Thanks to my wife for creating that kind of home with me, and having to put up with the worst along the way. I'll cook dinner for you tonight, I promise.

Beauty and Chaos

Lastly, I'd like to thank Tokyo. That is maybe a weird thing to do, sort of like an adult writing a letter to Santa Claus. Tokyo is an imaginary construct, of course, and does not really exist in any single place or in any exact way. It's a city whose hugeness refuses even metaphoric understanding. Tokyo slips through words like water through a net, or to use the Buddhist metaphor, writing about it is like catching fish with a hollow gourd. Just the same, I hope I've caught at least some sort of small fish, yet it's probably the feeling of thanks here that will slip away fastest back into the watery immensity of the city.

If you enjoyed these essays, please consider writing a quick review to recommend the collection to other readers. I would appreciate it, and I thank you in advance!

Glossary

abunai—"It's dangerous!" often shouted by mothers to children

agaru—to go up

arubaito—part-time job

asari—a lighter flavor of ramen noodles

bento—lunch box, or boxed lunch

bonenkai—year end parties, literally 'forget the year party'

bonsai—a miniature potted plant, trimmed and cared for carefully

bosozoku—motorcycle gangs

bottle keep—a system for keeping your own bottle at a bar

center-gai—the main street in Shibuya, with lots of young people

chashu—the slice of meat often put into ramen noodles

chikan—a pervert who grabs women on trains or streets

Chiyoda Line—one of the important subway lines

Beauty and Chaos

chome—a marker of space, like a city block only not linear

chukka—an informal place to eat Chinese style food

Chuo Line—the central east-west line through the middle of Tokyo

daikon—a type of long, white radish

dame—bad, or wrong, or impossible

depachika—food market on the bottom floor of a department store

Don Quixote—cheap chain store selling everything

ekiden—relay race

   fureeta—a full-time part-time worker, from "free arubaito"

furo, ofuro—bath

furoshiki—a cloth for wrapping things

gairaigo—a word imported from abroad

ganbatte—good luck, go for it, a word to encourage people

Genji Monogatari—"The Tale of Genji," famous novel from the 11th century

genkan—the entryway area of a house

Ginza—one of the fanciest, ritziest areas in Tokyo

Glossary

giri—obligation, social debt

gochisosama—"thank you for the meal," said at the end of a meal or when someone pays for you

gomen nasai—"I'm sorry," words used as apology in many situations

gomi—trash, garbage

gyudon—a common meal of fried beef on rice

Hachiko crossing—the most famously crowded four-way crosswalk, in Shibuya

haiku—poem of 17 syllables, with a precise 5-7-5 structure

Harajuku—trendy, fashionable area of Tokyo

hiragana—one of the alphabets of Japanese language

ikebana—flower arranging

Ikebukuro—one of the bigger and livelier areas of Tokyo

ima doko desu ka?—"where are you right now?"

Inokashira Line—a train line in western Tokyo

irrashaimase—"Welcome," called out to customers entering a shop

izakaya—one type of drinking restaurant

Kabukicho—the red light district in Shinjuku

Beauty and Chaos

kanji—Chinese characters, one of the basic writing systems

kare-sansui—dry rock garden, usually in Zen temples

katakana—another alphabet, usually for foreign words

kawaii—cute or adorable, but much more than that, too

KDDI—one of the telecommunication companies

kendo—a style of martial arts using swords

Kichijoji—trendy area in western Tokyo

kimono—traditional style of garment

kissaten—coffee shop

koban—police box, found all over the city

Koenji—an area in western Tokyo

kotteri—a flavor for ramen, oily and thick

Kyoto—after Tokyo, the most famous city, very traditional

ma—many meanings, but here a pause or silent moment

manga—Japanese style comics

manga kissaten—a coffee shop where you can read comics

meishi—name card or shop card

menma—pickled bamboo shoots, often added to ramen

Glossary

mingei—folk art

miso—fermented bean paste, used as a seasoning

moshi-moshi—"hello"

mottainai—wasteful, but with the feeling of sinful or too much so

Narita Airport—the main international airport in Tokyo

natsubate—summer fatigue, common symptom in the humid summer

natto—fermented soy beans, loved and hated

NHK—the main public broadcasting station

nihonjinron—a genre of texts focusing on Japanese identity, culture or nationality

nihonshu—a more formal name for Japanese sake, or rice wine

nijikai—after party, literally "the second place"

ninjo—human feeling, desire, passion, as opposed to giri, obligation

nomiya—literally 'drinking place'

nonbiri—daydreaming, relaxing, being comfortable

noren—short curtain outside a restaurant or shop

Beauty and Chaos

Obon—holiday in August, returning home or to ancestor's graves

ofuro, furo—a bath

OL—from 'office lady,' a female secretary or office worker

omiyage—a souvenir, usually a gift.

onsen—a hot springs for bathing, often a hotel or resort

osoji—big cleaning, like spring cleaning

oyayubi-zoku—slightly out of date term for cellphone addicts

pachinko—vertical pinball game, but a form of gambling

ramen—noodles, can be many kinds

romaji—another alphabet, with Roman letters, usually for foreign words

ronin—masterless samurai, also for students retaking entrance exams

Ryoanji—famous Zen rock garden temple in Kyoto

sake—Japanese rice wine

sakura—cherry blossoms, cherry trees

sashimi—raw fish, usually eaten without rice

senpai—elder person at school or a company, mentor

shacho—section chief in a company

Glossary

Shibuya—one of the liveliest areas in Tokyo

shinhatsubai—newly on sale, a term for the most recent product

Shinjuku—one of the largest and busiest areas of Tokyo

shiokara—salted fish guts, usually squid, eaten raw, salted and fermented

shita—down

shitamachi—"lower town" the area of eastern Tokyo which is older

shochu—distilled rice wine, a strong alcoholic drink

shoji—traditional sliding door usually with paper covering

shoyu—soy sauce

soba—a more Japanese style of noodle, different from ramen

sodai gomi—oversize trash, must be paid to be picked up

soto—outside, physically or socially

Suica card—electronic, automatic train pass card

sumimasen—usually means "I'm sorry," but also to interrupt, get attention politely

tachi-yomi—standing reading, one of many "tachi-" activities

Beauty and Chaos

tadaima—called out when returning home

takuhaibin—delivery service, Japan's services are extensive

tatami—woven mats

tebasaki—chicken wings, common dish

tempura—battered, deep fried food, almost anything can be tempura

Tokaido—the traditional road connecting Tokyo and Kyoto

torii—traditional Japanese style gate, usually in front of Shinto shrine

tsukemen—a style of noodles dipped in sauce

uchi—inside, physically or socially

ue—up, above

washi—traditional Japanese paper

yakitori—fried chicken skewers, but also vegetables and other things

Yamanote Line—the central, circular line in Tokyo

yatai—a movable food stall, set up at night on street corners

Zen—Zen is Zen

Dedication

This book, of course, is dedicated to my wife.

Also by Michael Pronko, look for:

Tokyo's Mystery Deepens
Motions and Moments

And forthcoming, Tokyo mystery/thrillers:

The Last Train
Tokyo Hand

More info at:
www.michaelpronko.com

About jazz in Tokyo:
www.jazzinjapan.com

About the author

I have lived, taught and written in Tokyo for fifteen years. I work as a professor at Meiji Gakuin University teaching American literature, film, music, and art. Fielding questions from my students about Jackson Pollock or Kurt Vonnegut and then wandering through Shinjuku's neon chaos always pops ideas for writing into my head.

I have written for a batch of publications in Japan. I've worked at The Japan Times for a dozen years, the once-great Tokyo Q, for a learner-oriented weekly ST Shukan, Winds Magazine, Jazz Colo[u]rs (in Italian!), Artscape Japan (check it out for great art reviews) and have run my own website Jazz in Japan (jazzinjapan.com) for almost a decade. I also helped found Japan's first bilingual jazz magazine, Jazznin and continue to publish academic articles and run a conference on teaching literature.

The essays in *Beauty and Chaos: Slices and Morsels of Tokyo Life* were originally published in Newsweek Japan in Japanese and collected together in a single volume in 2006. Two more collections followed, also in Japanese, *The Other Side of English—An Anti-Grammar Manifesto* and *Tokyo's Mystery Deepens*, both in 2009. The latter collection is also available in both Japanese and in English, and the former is out only in Japanese.

Their popularity here in Japan has led to my being invited for regular appearances on radio and TV programs for NHK (Japan's PBS) and Nihon TV's "The Most Useful School in the World," as well as several other places such as New York Channel One. It's very cool to video-fy the essays, but TV is a very different world.

I was born in Kansas City, also a very different world from Tokyo. After traveling several years, in and out of graduate school, I lived in Beijing, China for three years. Now, I live in western Tokyo with my wife, Lisa Yinghong Li, to whom this book is dedicated. She also teaches and writes.

If you enjoyed these essays, please consider writing a quick review to recommend the collection to other readers. I would appreciate it, and I thank you in advance!

www.ingramcontent.com/pod-product-compliance
Lightning Source LLC
Chambersburg PA
CBHW021142080526
44588CB00008B/169